BASES

EMPIRE

A CHART OF AMERICAN EXPANSION

By GEORGE MARION

THIRD EDITION • NEW MATERIAL

FAIRPLAY PUBLISHERS

25 WEST 44th STREET • NEW YORK 18, N. Y.

For information address Fairplay Publishers, 25 W. 44th St., N. Y. 18.

Printed in the U.S.A. First edition, April 1, 1948.
Second edition with new material, November 15, 1948.
Third edition with new material, February 15, 1949.

209

PREFACE

This preface would be unnecessary if speech were really free in our country today. But it isn't. The House un-American Activities Committee is publicly rewriting the Bill of Rights. And my experiences with this book suggest that there is some hidden revision going on, too.

No commercial publisher was willing to publish the book because it was on the "wrong" side of a bitterly controversial question in a climate of national political intolerance. When I published Bases & Empire myself, the watchdogs of Big Business would not let me enter the market-place to sell it. The *New York Times,* for instance, refused point-blank to accept paid advertisements for the book. (Later, the "liberal" *New York Star* — ex-*PM* — did the same.) As the *Times* book section strongly influences the market, I took the trouble of appealing the verdict to publisher Arthur Hays Sulzberger and managing editor Edwin James. They declined to reverse the finding or to give any reason for their act of political censorship.

In effect, our secret rulers simply banned the book. But it wasn't just a book that was denied freedom of the press: it was a point of view. Today's witch-hunters have only to pin horrendous labels on me and my work as a sufficient "reason" for denying me the protection of the Bill of Rights. But what about *you* who are thus denied the right to hear me speak? What reason can our hidden censors give for putting your mind in protective custody?

The question is pertinent because my book is not at all designed for specialists in politics. It addresses itself to the average American, or rather, to virtually every American. What it tries to prove is this:

A Wall Street clique has seized control of our country. The clique, and its allies in the armed forces, want similar control of the entire globe. To that end, they are trying to force United States military power (the armor of economic power) into every corner of the earth. The effort has already provoked half a dozen civil wars and it surely promises to provide a third world war.

This, of course, contradicts the official theory underlying United States foreign and domestic policies today. According to that theory, the world is going to hell in a handbasket because Russia likes it that way. On the basis of evidence from "respectable" (i.e., anti-Soviet) sources, the book refutes that theory. It supplies evidence that the responsibility for today's world tension rests on the former bankers and Wall Street lawyers who are now our leading "statesmen."

Certainly that is not a popular view today. But I think it would be if the facts got a chance. That's why I wrote the book. It is a plea for fair public debate of vital world issues. It asks that the average American get a chance to hear the facts presented by opponents of the "contain Russia" policy.

I hope the facts in the book will persuade you to say "No" to the Truman Doctrine and the Marshall Plan, induce you to say "Get out and stay out" to the banker-general-admiral regime in Washington. But above all I hope the book will enable you to recognize the hand of imperialism in all the Red Menace propaganda that will assail us for years to come.

George Marion
November 1, 1948

CONTENTS

PART I: WORLDWIDE BASES

CHAPTER 1. HISTORY AND HOKUM, 7.

CHAPTER 2. OUR MILITARY EMPIRE, 15.

CHAPTER 3. ARMS AND THE PLAN, 24.

CHAPTER 4. CONQUEST OF POWER, 39.

CHAPTER 5. A HEMISPHERE FOR ONE, 49.

CHAPTER 6. AN AMERICAN LAKE, 57.

CHAPTER 7. THE GEM OF ALL OCEANS, 67.

PART II: BOUNDLESS EXPANSION

CHAPTER 8. PROFIT AND POWER, 76.

CHAPTER 9. THE OPEN DOOR, 87.

CHAPTER 10. DOLLAR DIPLOMACY, 99.

CHAPTER 11. THE DAIREN ALIBI, 117.

CHAPTER 12. DOMINATION WITHOUT ANNEXATION, 130.

CHAPTER 13. AMERICAN INFILTRATION, 144.

CHAPTER 14. CHART OF AMERICAN EMPIRE, 160.

PART III: TAKE YOUR CHOICE

CHAPTER 15. THE PRICE OF REACTION, 170

CHAPTER 16. THERE IS A WAY, 187

PART I: WORLDWIDE BASES

CHAPTER I

HISTORY AND HOKUM

Reader, relax. This book contains no blueprint for world peace. Its aim is the modest one of assembling some elementary facts that could help the average citizen to play his part in shaping American policy. The United States is a democracy and that makes each of us responsible, to some degree, for everything that happens in our country and for all that our country does abroad. Of course, you and I do not have as much actual influence over our government, as large a voice in determining its course, as do the Whitneys and Lamonts of the Morgan banking interests; John D. Rockefeller, Jr., whose power extends far beyond the family control of Standard Oil; or the Mellon and du Pont families with their multi-billion dollar aluminum, automotive, chemical and financial monopolies. We do, nevertheless, have a voice. Being many, we could come to be heard much more clearly and frequently if we chose to speak with one voice.

To do that, we should have to learn to see our common interest, despite the differences of occupation, national origin, skin-color, religion, and general psychological outlook that divide us today. After all, great rivalries mark the behind-the-scenes life of industry and finance, yet the bankers and industrialists have learned to protect their common interests even while settling their differences in, figuratively speaking, armed battle. Because they are few, it is much easier for them to solve this problem of overall unity that embraces conflict of interest. It will be harder for us. But we will gain much, democracy will gain much, by our mere effort to achieve that end.

A better knowledge of world affairs would help us to further our common purpose, or at any rate to see where our interests lie. The American people are constantly flattered that they are the best-informed people on earth. It is categorically untrue. We are merely the most-informed. More meaningless words are hurled at us daily, in more than 50,000,000 newspapers, on tens of thousands of radio programs, in thousands of magazines and hundreds of newsreel commentaries, than any other people has to put up with. Almost all the facts of domestic and international affairs are to be found among these billions of daily words. But it is a fulltime job simply to read enough papers, magazines and books to have some basis of comparing the various views presented, and it requires special training to put current events against the background of history to obtain a valid meaning. Our information industries make no effort whatsoever to provide this consistent meaning that can alone enlighten.

Such an insane profusion of words can misinform or confuse; it cannot inform. The news industry and the other opinion-forming trades are not organized to educate us. They see us only as customers. If we buy more papers, they can sell more advertising at higher rates and make more money. A wealth of sensational stories, or of events distorted by emphasis on unusual but minor aspects — headlines, in other words — will sell more papers than a sober style that reports, analyzes, and interprets the trend of each day's events.

Moreover, the confused end-product of the news-vending process is not purely accidental. Beyond their desire to sell papers and advertising, the opinion-makers are biased. Press, radio and movies are Big Business. The "information" industries are, in turn, an inseparable part of the larger industry-banking complex, all manipulated and controlled by a relative handful of Lamonts, Mellons, du Ponts and Rockefellers. In the conflict of interest between this small group with its tremendous influence on national policy, and the millions of ordinary Americans who have little to say, the opinion-forming industries are not neutral. They speak for the minority; they speak for the rich and powerful.

The few and powerful have always been afraid of the poor and many. Long before the day of expensive public relations counsel, the rich invented charity, patronized religion and the arts, distributed free bread and promoted free circuses so that wealth might be associated with virtue and generosity instead of with usury and slavery. In the same tradition, the opinion-forming industries of our time shudder at the word "capitalism," avoid all evidence that there is a conflict of classes within the country or that the United States participates in a Great Power struggle for worldwide place, power and profit. Under their influence, the current public discussion of America's role in the world is conducted on an absurd and infantile level. There is nothing in it that can enlighten the average man. It contains little reference to the realities of markets and monopolies but talks a great deal about some intangible thing called "American moral leadership."

In his first general review of foreign affairs after assuming the Presidency, Mr. Truman on October 25, 1945 laid down twelve moral principles and said they were, in effect, our foreign policy. The whole high tone is summed up in the first point of the statement of principles:

"We seek no territorial expansion or selfish advantage. We have no plans for aggression against any other state, large or small. We have no objective which need clash with the peaceful aims of any other nation."

This impressive statement was relied upon officially throughout the severe international tension of 1945-1948 as an adequate explanation and justification of American foreign policy. Of course our objectives "need not" clash with the peaceful aims of any other nation. Provided, that is, they take the same view of our objectives as our officials and newspapers do. For example, we publicly proclaim that we and we alone shall rule Japan during the occupation period. In the event there are differences of opinion among the powers, "the view of the United States shall prevail." Now, should one of the powers feel that our rule, in effect, incorporates Japanese resources and manpower and strategic territory into a purely United States-controlled military apparatus, that *"need not"* be a source of friction. The dissatisfied power has only to keep its mouth shut, and there will be no friction.

Behind the now world-debated Truman Doctrine and Marshall Plan lies this arrogant assumption of our own moral perfection. The bi-partisan backers of the Plan sell it as a barrier to what is supposed to be the imminent peril of Communist expansion. But their insistence on the "peril" would be incomplete if it were not matched by a smug confidence that our inner purity makes it perfectly all right to push our own power anywhere in the world to ward off the "threat."

That wouldn't constitute expansion. Why? Because we have appointed ourselves champions of the rights of small nations. We are the knights of self-determination. We bring free elections and food to all nations. When we use what Secretary Marshall has described as "the greatest military power and military resources ever assembled" in this way, it is out of pure altruism. It is not done "to acquire for the United States a special privileged position, either political or economic" (again in the words of General Marshall). No, we do it simply because that's the kind of world we like to live in. We don't ask a thing for ourselves. We are just a big brother to all mankind.

Our foreign policy amounts to the simple assertion that the United States can do no wrong. That is the inevitable effect of the high moral tone. It leaves the realm of reality where interests of nations and individuals do, in fact, conflict. It creates an imaginary world in which one nation is endowed with both supreme power and supreme wisdom. Wherever an American pursues a material interest abroad, wherever an American corporation claims the right to lay a pipeline, sink a well, plant rubber, establish an airline or make an investment, Americans arms and the State Department go along to polish the halo. The suggestion that every such business venture should be fully publicized, have its facts aired, is treated as an offense to our national honor.

This incredibly childish doctrine especially precludes discussion of objectives pursued by the government itself, notably air, naval and military bases in various parts of the world. President Truman's first principle of foreign policy appears to have been modified, in practice, to read rather like a speech by Tom Sawyer: "We seek no territorial expansion or selfish advantage except maybe a few battered old bases that nobody else wants and that aren't much good anyhow." A *Times** editorial on June 17, 1946, after a protestation that "neither the United States nor Great Britain can be charged with aggrandizement," rewords this studiously naive view of our base demands:

"Though the United States seeks additional bases in regions formerly under the control of, or accessible to, the enemy, it does so either in sparsely populated islands incapable of statehood or self-government, or by agreement with like-minded countries, withdrawing whenever, as in the case of the Azores, consent is withheld."

But it so happens we didn't withdraw from the Azores.

---

* The *New York Times* will be referred to throughout as the *Times*. I have quoted it repeatedly for several reasons: It devotes more space to foreign affairs than perhaps any other American daily; it speaks for and reflects so closely the policy of the men presently governing the country, that specialists must accept it as a semi-official rather than purely independent paper; and, finally, it affects to an extreme degree the pretense of Olympian detachment and "objectivity" characteristic of the American press. The *Times* presents the propaganda as well as the considered program of the most powerful American financial-industrial interests.

We stayed there, and on February 2, 1948 obtained Portuguese "consent" to military use of Lagens Airfield for another three to five years. The time limit is meaningless. As diplomats told *Times* correspondent Cyrus Sulzberger (dispatch from Lisbon dated November 21, 1948): "The United States can have an Azores base permanently on a temporary basis."

The fact is we sent warships to Portugal to demonstrate that we would obtain her consent to our use of the Azores — or else. And we obtained what we wanted, in a veiled form, because, as Portugal's dictator, Dr. Salazar, told a *Times* correspondent at that very time, Portugal had passed to the United States sphere of influence! These are facts pertinent to any adult discussion. There can be no intelligent discussion if it is to be assumed, as a starting point, that there is nothing to discuss; that there is no need to go into the facts; that even if we demand bases on the territory of sixty other countries, the spiritual influence of American policy is a guarantee that everything will come out all right in the end. No decent person with the responsibility of conducting a business abroad, or handling foreign affairs, or making a study of actual world relations for academic purposes, can possibly take this pious drivel seriously.

"It should be taken as an axiom of diplomatic psychology that no nation can act consistently from motives of spiritual satisfaction," Professor Benjamin H. Williams remarks in *The Economic Foreign Policy of the United States*. "If the officials of any government pursue policies which sacrifice the national interest or involve the nation in commitments and entanglements without the hope of material gains, they are so fiercely set upon by adversely affected groups within the country that they are soon forced to change their policies or give way to another set of officers."

Secretary of State Charles Evans Hughes, later Chief Justice of the Supreme Court, remarked that "foreign policies are not built upon abstractions. They are the result of national interest arising from some immediate exigency . . ." Admiral Mahan — whose influence on American policy can hardly be overestimated — puts it even more sharply: "Self-interest is not only a legitimate, but a fundamental cause for national policy; one which needs no cloak of hypocrisy . . . [As Washington said] it is vain to expect governments to act continuously on any other ground than national interest. They have no right to do so, being agents and not principals."

Mahan was referring to Washington's warning in his Farewell Address, "that it is folly in one nation to look for distinterested favors from another . . . There can be no greater error than to expect or calculate upon real favors from nation to nation. It is an illusion which experience must cure, which a just pride ought to discard." In a 1778 letter, Washington said it is a maxim "founded on the universal experience of mankind, that no nation is to be trusted farther than it is bound by its own interests; and no prudent statesman or politician will venture to depart from it."

Nor have our statesmen and politicians departed from it — except in words. They have acquired the habit of gilding our material interests with "moral" phrases. Realists have persistently fought this tendency because it confuses not alone the public but the men responsible for the formulation and execution of national policy. F. M. Huntington Wilson, Department of State career man and Undersecretary of State in the time of President Taft, deplored "our national foible for grandiloquent sentimentality" and himself compiled a hardboiled textbook for dollar diplomats under the revealing title: *The Relation of Government to Foreign Investment.*

Commodore Perry was annoyed with the phrasemongers who presented his forcible opening of Japan in spiritual terms — terms comparable to those now employed by Winston Churchill and John Foster Dulles in their campaign to build a European bloc under the guise of "saving European civilization." Said Perry: "Of the selfishness of our motives we readily admit that we sought commercial intercourse with Japan because we supposed it would be advantageous. . . . We can only smile at the simplicity of those who expect to deceive the world by profession of pure, disinterested friendship from one nation toward another, irrespective of all considerations of national benefit."

Let it be said emphatically: these blunt affirmations of American pursuit of material interest are not here presented as an accusation of any kind. A like demonstration of material foundation for policy might be made for any country in the world. The highest spokesmen of the Soviet Union, for instance, have replied over a long period of years, to questions about the "orientation" of Soviet foreign policy, that Soviet policy was not "orientated" on the East or on the West, not on Germany or on France, "but on the Soviet Union alone." It is neither good nor bad that nations should base their policies on material self-interest; it is neither moral nor immoral nor amoral. It is simply an elementary fact from which all meaningful discussion must start.

Let us, therefore, leave worthless "moral" arguments and get down to the bread-and-butter, dollars-and-cents, what's-in-it-for-me, material realities. In this case, our starting point is a simple tabulation of the facts concerning American bases abroad. Once we have these facts, we can appraise our own policy more objectively. We can see it as it looks to other nations. Applying the same hardboiled standards to their policies, we should be able to see where our material interests meet and where they conflict. No doubt we can then find a basis of compromise out of which a reciprocal toleration and a mutual respect can grow. Is not a firm peace, resting on the solid ground of national interest, worth more than the pigheaded pursuit of some alleged "high principle" that really spells war?

CHAPTER 2

OUR MILITARY EMPIRE

The little old bases we are admittedly seeking are commonly supposed to be a rather minor group of islands vaguely known to the public as the Japanese-mandated islands of the Pacific. The former Japanese mandates are, however, no trifle. They number more than six hundred and are scattered over 3,000,000 square miles of the Pacific Ocean! They consist of the Marshalls, Carolinas and the Marianas or Ladrones, containing such war-familiar names as Truk, Palau, Ponape and Yap. Spanish possessions until 1898, they then passed to Germany and after World War I were mandated to Japan. Though the land area involved is but 829 square miles with a population of some 85,000, the mandated area runs 1,200 miles north from the Equator and extends 2,500 miles from east to west. It dominates an expanse of water sometimes put at 25,000,000 square miles.

All this is now a United Nations Trust Territory under absolute control of the United States. The Trust Territory, however, is not, as many believe, the core of the military-strategic assets claimed by the United States. The public has been poorly informed as to the true extent of American empire-building. It would be more precise to say that the truth has been carefully concealed from the public. *Times* correspondent James Reston, reporting from Washington on June 24, 1946, admits as much:

"Negotiations on the future of these bases in the two great oceans are now going on," he wrote. "Nothing is said about them officially, *and even publication of the fact of the negotiations is discouraged.*"

Perhaps this "iron curtain" explains how little the public, even the largest part of the American intelligentsia, understands the scope of American military commitments and ambitions. The strategic system we are setting up is literally global in scale, Reston reported. He said, in effect, that our negotiators were seeking sole American sovereignty over islands and continental bases sufficient to dominate the Atlantic and Pacific.

"American policy is now directed not toward an international solution of the problem (as favored by President Roosevelt) but toward the attainment of naval and air rights for the United States in the islands and major ports of the communities washed by two oceans."

We were (and are) asking not only Japanese islands but even possessions of our closest allies. Reston noted, for instance, that "we suggested to the British not United Nations bases in Canton and on Funafuti and Christmas Islands in the Pacific, but that these islands be handed over to American sovereignty." They were British possessions but they have since entered United States control, as planned.

In a dispatch on May 11, 1946, Reston had already reported that the three islands, once yielded to America, would become "part of a vast United States defense system in the Pacific, part of which would be run under United States sovereignty, part in collaboration with the British and other Pacific powers, and part under the Security and Trusteeship Councils of the United Nations." The United States intended, however, to restrict the British, Australians and New Zealanders to a secondary role. Our negotiators, Reston said, would decide which islands should become "sovereign territory," to form, along with present American possessions, a decisive chain of bases. Then the United States would be willing "to place some strategic islands under the Security Council of the United Nations on terms that could give us virtual sovereignty over them; and to place others under the Trusteeship Council of the United Nations when they are not of vital strategic importance."

This is clearer than clear. When the United States finally presented trusteeship proposals to the United Nations

General Assembly in November 1946, it followed the general pattern predicted by Reston. The United States, President Truman announced, would be sole administering authority, would retain exclusive military, naval and air rights, and would rule the islands as "an integral part of the United States."

But all of this over-emphasizes the Pacific. It is necessary to point out that we are equally seeking to convert the Atlantic into an American lake. As Reston puts it, our program calls for naval and air rights in the "major ports of the communities washed by the two oceans," that is, Asia, North and South America, Europe, Africa, and even Australia. In short, what we are seeking today is no handful of sparsely-inhabited coral islands whose people are "incapable of statehood or self-government," but a worldwide budget of bases.

The bases themselves are meaningful only in the context of a system of global power established by the United States during World War II. What we are demanding, broadly viewed, is not exactly new bases but the consolidation of the military empire acquired in the course of the past five or six years. The public, following the battles, grew familiar with strange place-names in every corner of the earth. It has yet to learn, however, how many of these names are now permanent features of American power-geography, rooted in a long history of overseas expansion. They add up to a global military-strategic empire, built so quietly that only skilled listeners could hear the carpenters at work.

It is precisely the size of this empire that American officials and our press appear determined to conceal. This was made embarrassingly evident in the first session of the United Nations General Assembly during debate on the Soviet proposal for a so-called "troop census." The Russians asked for an accounting of all bases and troops held by member nations on non-enemy soil. They readily agreed to a counter-proposal that home forces be included. At that point the American delegation inspired parliamentary maneuvers which barely staved off passage of the resolution.

Why? Because, as Reston frankly described it, an American accounting would have revealed "the fact that United States and British troops were scattered all over the globe." He said: "The list reads like a gazetteer. . . . A review of the location of troops of the major United Nations shows that the United States has by far the largest number of overseas expeditions on foreign soil at the present time. . . . We would have to report not only on our troops in China, Egypt, India and Iceland, but on our bases in the British Atlantic islands, in Greenland, the British Commonwealth islands in the Pacific, and in the islands and territories of the Latin American republics."

Reston, of course, was far from exaggerating. The location of American troops, as revealed by the War Department six months after the end of the war, was a rough map of our world system of bases, valid today. The department listed some sixty countries and island groups, including the strange entry, "Africa," as the only clue to our positions on that vast continent.

Listed in this hemisphere were: Alaska, Canada, Costa Rica, Cuba, Jamaica, Nassau, Haiti, Puerto Rico, St. Thomas, Trinidad, British Guiana, Bermuda, French Guiana, Newfoundland, Brazil. Despite the length of the list, it was not complete. Tiny news-items ever since that time report negotiations to retain wartime bases and even acquire new ones, in hemisphere countries strangely omitted from the list. Among these are Guatemala, Peru, Ecuador and the Republic of Panama.

The Atlantic list showed American troops in Greenland, the Azores, Iceland, England, Ascension Island, Liberia; while in Europe and the Mediterranean area, these countries were named: Belgium, Norway, France, Luxembourg, Germany, Austria, Hungary, Czechoslovakia, Bulgaria, Italy,

French Morocco, Tunisia and Egypt. If Hungary, Czechoslovakia, Bulgaria and Italy may now be removed from the list, the tabulation stretches in new directions: Greece, Turkey, and Iran must be added. American strategic claims, moreover, are evident now in Syria, Lebanon, Iraq, Palestine, Yemen and Saudi Arabia as well as Egypt.

In the Pacific and Asia, the list showed American troops in China, Japan, Korea, Formosa, the Philippines, Ryukyus, Carolines, Marshalls, Marianas, Admiralties, Bonins, Marcus, Solomons, Fijis, Aleutians and Hawaiians; in New Caledonia, Wake, Phoenix, Midway, Christmas; in Australia, Borneo, Burma and India.

This global distribution of American power was a product of World War II. But it is not necessary for me to "prove" that it represents pretty much what our rulers and would-be rulers insist on retaining forever. "Proof" is unnecessary because our Big Navy and Air Force and Army spokesmen keep repeating it aloud. For example, Struve Hensel, Assistant Secretary of Navy, outlined that service's views at a press conference on September 5, 1945. He said, in the words of the Associated Press, that we should "retain a vast postwar ring of naval bases spanning the Pacific, including one base that was formerly British."

For the Navy alone and quite independently of what the Army and Air Force might want, Mr. Hensel demanded nine major bases in the Pacific, "stretching from the Aleutians to the Admiralties," and also "six permanent major bases in the Atlantic, including one on Bermuda and another at Argentia, Newfoundland."

Mr. Hensel named the bases the Navy wanted for the Pacific as Kodiak; Adak; Hawaii; Guam-Saipan-Tinian considered as one; Balboa in the Canal Zone; Iwo Island in the Bonin and Volcano groups; Manus in the Admiralties (British before the war); the Philippines; and Okinawa in the Ryukyus. For the Atlantic, Argentia; Bermuda; Roosevelt

Roads, Puerto Rico; San Juan, Puerto Rico; Guantanamo Bay, Cuba; Coco Sola, Canal Zone.

This is far from telling all that Mr. Hensel actually revealed about United States territorial ambitions as represented by the military-strategic demands of a single service. In addition to the nine major bases in the Pacific, Mr. Hensel said the Navy wanted many, many others kept "not as essential to the Navy's needs but primarily to prevent them from being used by any other nation." He cited Wake, Midway, Eniwetok (later converted into an atomic proving ground), Kwajalein and Truk in this category, but gave no overall number. He did give a hint, however, when he revealed that "at various times in the war," the United States had built 256 bases of all sizes and types in the Pacific Theater and 228 in the Atlantic, a total of 484 bases!

In the more than two years since Hensel outlined the Navy's plans, there has been no shrinkage in the claims of any of the armed services. At the end of 1947, *Times* military correspondent Hanson W. Baldwin, noting withdrawal of our troops from Italy under the terms of the peace treaty, said there were still 600,000 to 700,000 American soldiers and sailors overseas. His information shows that the "gazetteer" character of American military policy had not changed. Baldwin's December 14, 1947 article is worth summarizing.

He estimated that half of all U. S. regular forces were overseas. Of these, 226,000 represented forces aboard naval vessels outside continental waters; 130,000 to 145,000 occupation troops in Europe; about 160,000 in Japan and Korea.

The European force was put at 110,000 to 130,000 in Germany; 9,000 to 12,000 in Austria and 5,000 in Trieste.

Aside from actual troop figures, Baldwin conceded that there were other ways of establishing military-strategic claims, as by naval demonstrations in the Mediterranean. "Recent naval revelations," he added, "indicate that at least one small shore base is maintained temporarily near the Mediterranean area at Port Lyautey in Morocco, north of Casablanca."

Baldwin said there must be added to actual occupation forces, 60,000 to 70,000 sailors and marines at overseas bases in the Panama-Caribbean, Alaska-Aleutian, Hawaii, Marianas and Philippines-Okinawa areas.

"Thousands of other Americans," he said, "are scattered over large sections of the globe, chiefly in small detachments. There are several hundreds still in Greenland manning weather stations and small 'bases' which are now a subject of negotiation with Denmark.

"There are men on duty at weather and radar stations in northern Canada, on the River Clyde in Baffin Island and in the Alaska-Aleutian area. The smaller Pacific islands are peopled by isolated detachments of Army, Navy or Marine personnel—most of them connected with military government, weather stations or guard and 'housekeeping' duties."

A few days after Baldwin made this summary, it was announced that the United States had at last returned the Port Lyautey base to which he referred. But the announcement failed to mention that the return took place only after France had agreed to let the U.S. Navy retain "landing rights" there. This is one more reminder that formal cession or lease of bases to the United States is not the sole test of American military infiltration; nor is formal "return" of wartime bases an indication of the shrinking of the American strategic empire.

Far from shrinking, our chain of bases in the Mediterranean was growing rapidly at that very time. The United States set up again in January the air base it had maintained during wartime at Mellaha in Libya (near Tripoli) and the British announced that American military planes would be granted use of British fields in that region beginning with Royal Air Force bases at Castel Benito, Libya, and Luqa, Malta. Hanson Baldwin added a footnote to this on January 18. He said our fleet had visited Suda Bay, in Crete, a number of times and it "might be considered a potential naval base." But we don't really lack Mediterranean bases, he added, "for the British base at Cyprus and strong British positions at Malta and Gibraltar in addition to ports in British-held Libya are available to us." For that matter, he said, American heavy bombers are still being "rotated" to Europe and operated from bases not only in Germany but in Britain. Of course no one needs to be reminded of this fact since the artificial "Berlin crisis" that began in March 1948. So many heavy bombers were moved to British bases, that a real war panic spread throughout the United Kingdom. Under cover of the cooked-up crisis, the United States returned to full possession and operation of the briefly surrendered wartime airfield at Burtonwood, Lancashire, where 30,000 Americans were based during the war. Aside from the effect on the British people of this operation, with its implication of American power to decide war or peace for England, the affair must have served as a new and bitter reminder to Britain's rulers that nowhere in the world is there a base the once mighty British imperialists can call their own.

At the other end of the world, about the same time, United States Army engineers were said to have completed a $13,000,000 American air base at Misawa near the northeast tip of Honshu Island. This was described publicly (for instance, a dispatch to the *Times* of May 3, 1948 from correspondent Lindesay Parrott) as but "the latest in a chain of airfields built at key points in Japan since the occupation began." The program makes no pretense of being part of the necessary police provisions for the occupying power, for Japan had plenty of military airfields. They were not, however, adapted to the biggest American bombers, and the new program was undertaken to correct this "defect."

These are but indications. No one outside high military or inner "bipartisan" planning councils of the government knows the real total of strategic positions directly and indirectly controlled by the United States through all three armed services plus various American-dominated native governments! How far can defense requirements go? It is revealing to discover that Admiral Raymond A. Spruance, Commander of the Fifth Fleet, had opposed postwar bases on Okinawa because that would spell something very different from "defense." Spruance told newsmen at Manila shortly before Struve Hensel included Okinawa in his list of major Navy bases: "It would be a sore point with us if a foreign power held a string of islands blockading our coast."

As much can be said of many other sites than Okinawa. It is simply impossible to keep increasing the number of any nation's bases indefinitely, and extending the range of its strategic positions over two-thirds of the globe, without converting "defense" into strategic empire with all the risks of empire. And that is what we have done. In the eyes of every people in the world — except the American people, flooded with misleading information by our "free press" — the following are the minimum limits of American strategic empire today:

1. We have acquired total strategic domination over the American hemisphere, beyond early effective challenge by any other Great Power.

2. We have taken over control of the Atlantic and Pacific Oceans.

3. We seek the necessary positions in Europe and Asia and Africa and Australasia to maintain that control. In practice, we have those positions as a result of occupation during the war. The pre-war possessors of the bases are in many cases unwilling to surrender them on our terms, but the United States continues in sole possession during endless negotiations. It is all very well to say that "we plot no conquests," but what if we refuse to surrender other people's territories loaned to us during the war?

CHAPTER 3

ARMS AND THE PLAN

The most sensational and revealing book anyone could dream up today, would be a full official record of all United States negotiations for bases since the war's end. Publication of that record would undo all the high moral propaganda we have been deluged with. In every part of the world, behind an alert censorship, our officials have negotiated to retain bases set up during the war and to establish new ones. But only when circumstances produce a crisis somewhere in the world over the issue of American bases, does the bare fact of the negotiations get through the iron curtain our "free press" has erected or accepted.

Our refusal to get out of Greenland has been the subject of bitter internal fights in Denmark, but the American people cannot be blamed if they do not know this. It is given so little press notice, when it is recorded at all, that they are unaware we have all but refused point-blank to get out of Greenland and return that possession to nominally sovereign Denmark. The *Times* gave ten lines on page 18, May 22, 1946, to a demand in the Danish parliament for termination of the wartime treaty with the United States by which we got into Greenland in the first place. Diplomatic "negotiations," in which we certainly hold more than one club over little Denmark's head, were still in progress at the end of 1947.

A similar story might be told of unequal negotiations with Portugal for positions in the Azores, and we retained military air rights in Iceland, civilian in form, only by forcing a change in the Icelandic Government. This, incidentally, was one of the first cases of the now familiar process by which Communists, no matter how large their electoral following, are ousted from governments by American economic and diplomatic pressure — with bombers and battleships in plain sight.

Since our military-strategic ambitions have the range of a gazetteer, a full account of our pressure-negotiations would run to encyclopedia size. A fair compromise would be to describe a typical case. The history of our negotiations with Panama fills the bill.

By treaty with Panama in 1942, we acquired 134 base sites on her soil, quite apart from the 10-mile canal strip which was not in question. The treaty specified that we would get out of Panama, give up all the bases, a year after the end of the war. American officials, seeking extension of the base agreement after the war, contended that the war wasn't over until a definitive treaty had been signed with Japan.

Now the United States, which so energetically denounced Russia for negotiating with "little" Iran while Russian troops were on Iranian soil — under a similar wartime agreement — conducted negotiations with much littler Panama under conditions far less equal. The United States proposed a number of permanent bases in Panama, particularly a base large enough to accommodate our biggest bombers at Rio Hato, on the Pacific side of Panama, seventy miles from the canal. The American proposal, especially with regard to the projected $30,000,000 development at Rio Hato, was that Panama grant the United States a lease for at least sixty and possibly ninety-nine years.

Such a lease is, in reality, not a lease at all: it is cession of the territory involved. On November 28, 1947, the United States Circuit Court of Appeals said as much in a decision involving a United States ninety-nine year base at Bermuda. Bermuda is a British possession but the court ruled that the leased base was in effect as much an American "possession" as Alaska, Hawaii, and Puerto Rico are. Examining the terms of the lease, the court said:

"The cumulative effect of these various provisions compels the conclusion that the areas are subject to fully as complete control by the United States as obtains in other areas long known as 'possessions' of the United States."

For sixteen months the United States pressed negotiations with Panama for concessions which, therefore, would have impaired the sovereignty of that state. The "free press" of the United States, very busy with alarming tales of Russian expansion, vaguely and barely reported the fact of negotiations but completely concealed the terms proposed by the United States. To my knowledge, none of the following facts got into print while the negotiations were in progress:

Foreign Minister Ricardo Alfaro vigorously opposed the American demands and characterized them as an attempt on Panamanian sovereignty. During the Inter-American Conference in Rio de Janeiro in August 1947, Secretary Marshall suggested to Alfaro that he might consider fifty years, or, later, thirty. Alfaro replied that the sum of the terms would still add up to a loss of sovereignty for Panama.

On October 8, when General Marshall and Senor Alfaro were both attending the United Nations General Assembly in New York, Marshall suggested that the thirty years might be divided into a fifteen-year period followed by a fifteen-year option. He then made a "last" offer of ten and ten. Alfaro countered with two years and then raised his maximum to five. He left no doubt in Marshall's mind that he would quit office rather than sign a treaty on United States terms.

The State Department, however, counted on American economic influence in Panama to win compliance from that government in the long run. The $430,000 paid annually for lease of the Canal Zone, the $45,000 proposed annual fee for the base sites to be retained, and the money spent in developing the bases, added up to a very important influence in the economy of so small a country. (Though dollar-minded gentlemen never seem to perceive human sensibilities: one of the most irritating aspects of United States policy in Panama, was a kind of Jim Crow double-standard by which we paid American employes in gold and Panamanians in silver). Confident of our strength, the Department delivered on November 10, 1947, a note that — in view of the size of the two nations and the history of our seizure of Panama — amounted to an ultimatum. The Department called it a firm "final stand."

All this made no headlines here. But it roused popular fury in Panama. The government of that country nevertheless agreed to General Marshall's treaty terms and an agreement calling for a ten year lease on Rio Hato and other sites, with ten year renewal option, was prepared. Alfaro resigned in protest on December 9, but the treaty was signed the following day. Mass protest demonstrations and banners denouncing American imperialism marked the signature and continued, despite police violence, during subsequent consideration of the treaty by the National Assembly.

This at last broke through the barrier of silence maintained by the American press. It obtained limited space — as "riots" by "mobs," of course. The "riots," however, so truly represented Panamanian national sentiment that, against all the pressure the United States could bring to bear, the Assembly on December 22 unanimously repudiated the treaty! Not until then did the case of Panama finally win full headlines here!

The United States thereupon decided to withdraw from Panama. The *Times'* James Reston, a virtual spokesman for State Department circles, put it this way:

"The United States was not prepared to go before the United Nations and argue against a unanimous vote of the Parliament of a sovereign nation. . . . Otherwise, the whole moral argument against Soviet tactics in the Dardanelles, Iran and Eastern Europe would have been challenged, and nobody here was prepared to pay that price for the bases, *especially since the Administration is confident that we will eventually reach a mutually satisfactory arrangement with Panama."*

Administration confidence is, no doubt, increased by the fact that American control of the key bases has never been interrupted. When American military personnel left, arrangements were promptly made to move in "civilian" personnel. Pan American Airways, it was explained, had installed aerophares — navigation aids — which had been operated by the U.S. Army for the benefit of American military and commercial airlines. Following evacuation, the airline — an arm of the American government — assigned its own men to stations at Rio Hato, San Blas Point and Rey Island. Thus United States control of the facilities continues until such time as Panama has quieted down and its government can give away the bases without an uprising.

It is hard to pass this by without extended analysis of the way our press handled the whole affair. But I shall limit myself to a single point. Suppose Russia were negotiating with, say Turkey, for bases, and a Turkish president had approved an agreement. Then, as the treaty went to the Turkish parliament for approval, four thousand women marched in the streets to protest the agreement. Is there an American paper that wouldn't find room on the front page for that, even if there were a local earthquake story? But it happened in Panama, and the treaty was with the United States, so I found the story buried in the *Times* (December 17, 1947). It got eight lines under a one-line head.

No matter how well our "free press" may conceal such stories from us, ordinary, unscholarly people all over the world know about the Panama affair. They know that the people of Panama poured out into the streets celebrating the rejection of the treaty as they might have celebrated victory against an armed invader. Much as the defenders of Verdun and Madrid halted the enemy with the cry of, "They shall not pass," so the Panamanians rejoiced in the streets with the cry of, "It did not pass." And that is known everywhere. And the knowledge shapes world opinion of American policy.

THE ARMS RACE

It is our bases and our aggressive base-procurement policy that impresses the rest of the world. It does not matter how earnestly we explain that the Marshall Plan is strictly peaceful and absolutely unselfish, others will still see the bases. If we now add the impression created by the size of our arms budget, do we really believe we can convince anyone that our policy is one of "peaceful reconstruction?" We may re-christen the Marshall Plan the European Reconstruction Program, but the facts about our bases-and-armaments race will still contradict the name.

What an arms program it is! The unprecedented $10,-500,000,000 to $13,000,000,000 regularly appropriated for the armed services and related "national defense" needs in 1947, is a bare beginning. Absolutely fantastic sums were demanded as the new Congress met early in 1948. It does not in the least matter which of these demands succeed and which fail or how they are modified before they are realized. Their existence demonstrates to world opinion that our natinal policy is geared to virtually unlimited war preparations for the years ahead.

This outline of a total war-economy was drawn by the President's Air Policy Commission in a report submitted in January 1948 after hearings late in 1947. It particularly approved Air Force demands that would require us, first, to maintain a world chain of bomber-bases, and second, an air fleet as costly as our present twenty-billion-dollar Navy! In general, it recommended a bristling military program that would, the report said, increase our annual military expenses until, by 1952, they would be at least double their present enormous figure. Budget figures submitted by President

Truman giving "revised" estimates for 1948 and first estimates for 1949 only hint at the appalling totals even for the current year.

He asked for $10,746,000,000 for "national defense" in 1948 and $11,025,000,000 in 1949. "International affairs," which means our aggressive foreign policy, will cost $5,533,-000,000 for 1948 and $7,009,000,000 for 1949. For these two items alone, then, we are asked to provide $34,313,000,000 in two years. The thirty-four billions, incidentally, cover the Marshall Plan costs but not those of the Truman Doctrine, for in submitting his figures Mr. Truman indicated he would ask later for money to be used in Greece and China.

Nor does "national defense" cover all the essentially military expenditures. It is no easy matter to interpret the budget or the Air Policy Commission's report, but Hanson Baldwin estimated that by 1952 we would be called upon to lay out $25,000,000,000 a year for arms alone! "International affairs" and other indirect armaments expenditures would be extra! What the armaments program itself contemplates, is suggested by the following sample proposals, all made public by competent authorities:

1. Expenditure of five billions in the next few years for "redesign and improvement of atomic weapons." This is on the authority of David Lilienthal, chairman of the Atomic Energy Commission.

2. An overall expenditure, beyond reliable estimate, for a vast air program. This program, approved by the Air Policy Commission, was publicly formulated by Gen. Carl Spaatz, commander of the U.S. Air Force and W. Stuart Symington, Secretary of the Department of the Air Force, in hearings before the commission.

Spaatz and Symington called for at least 630 of our largest bombers (B-29s now and B-36s when available) to be based overseas ready to strike any part of the world, "in retaliation" for an attack, of course. There would be at least ten times that many lighter supporting craft in the air force they outlined, and a reserve force exceeding even this combined figure.

The number and composition of the "seventy groups" demanded by Spaatz and Symington, of which fifty-five are guaranteed by earlier appropriations, mean a peacetime Air Force (aside from Navy planes) of more than 20,000 aircraft. The report said on this score: "We have concluded that the minimum force necessary at the present time is an Air Force composed of 12,400 modern planes . . . and an adequate reserve, now estimated at 8,100 aircraft . . ."

It is also indicated that the Air Force has most of these planes except that its reserve is smaller than it would wish. What is particularly new in the program, as approved by the Air Policy Commission, is the demand for more money to place larger replacement orders each year so that the plane-manufacturing industry may be kept, if not on a war-footing, at least ready for quick expansion to war levels.

3. An overall "defense" program whose real cost cannot be estimated, in which the above-described expanded Air Force would be a key element. The nearest available cost figure is provided by the combined testimony of Acting Secretary of State Robert A. Lovett and plane designer Alexander P. de Seversky. Commenting on the program sketched by Lovett, Seversky said:

"The creation of these striking and defense forces in terms of tomorrow's potential and tomorrow's strategy may require an investment of national wealth approaching the value of our present fleet-in-being—that is to say, around $20,000,000,000, this over and above the current requirements of our present air forces as indicated by the Secretary of Air."

4. Denying the supremacy of the independent Air Force, John L. Sullivan, Secretary of the Department of the Navy, asked that the Navy's separate air force be set at 3,300 combat aircraft, 2,700 aircraft in fleet support, 2,000 training ships, 2,700 in reserve and 3,800 planes for spares

and overhaul work. To keep its force at this strength, the Navy would have to buy 2,500 to 3,000 new planes a year.

The report approved most of these demands: "The Navy requires 5,793 front-line planes, plus about 5,100 in support." Simple addition of these 10,893 Navy planes and 20,500 Air Force planes spells a peacetime combined combat airfleet of 31,393 planes! And the report, as well as a flock of military spokesmen, emphasize that this is just the figure for "Phase I," a preliminary period ending in 1952, when heaven knows what additions to the program will be made.

To reach even the Phase I level, the commission asked an expenditure on the Air Force alone of $4,150,000,000 in 1948. The combined aviation outlay for the year, another source reveals, would be $5,325,000,000. The commission's report appears to ask that this amount be increased to more than seven billions in 1949!

5. A guided missile program to cost staggering billions is an added starter. The first available figures to be made public on this program, were supplied by John K. Northrup, outstanding authority. He said 5,000 small guided missiles with a range of 600 miles would cost $375,000,000 to produce over a period of years; 5,000 1,400-mile supersonic missiles would cost $1,500,000,000; 5,000 giant ones with a top range of 3,500 miles, would take another $3,500,000,000. Nor is this entirely a matter of future projects. A number of agencies and services have long been conducting expensive research and development projects in this field.

6. Maintenance of 1,400,000 officers and men under arms in the several services. This would cost about $10,000,000,000 a year. But that doesn't include an annual cost of $765,000,000 for maintaining the National Guard at a strength of 723,000, with the help of Universal Military Training. UMT itself would cost two billions a year according to official estimates and double that by other — and possibly more reliable — estimates. The Army's Organized

Reserve Corps is another $400,000,000 and there is no estimate for that of the Navy; both mean, in effect, larger armed forces than the formal figure above.

7. Naval building centers on 80,000-ton carriers capable of launching 50-ton bombers. The Navy has under construction one battleship, two large aircraft carriers, two escort carriers, four heavy cruisers, two light cruisers, five destroyers, one submarine and ten small vessels. The budget-message calls for slowing down this construction, without abandoning it entirely, in order to emphasize new types of craft such as the super-carriers.

You do not have to go abroad to see what an impression this program produces on a mind not paralyzed by one-sided propaganda in its favor. A letter from a D. Molony in nearby Staten Island to the *Times* Sunday magazine of December 28, 1947, tells volumes in a few lines. The letter commented on an earlier article purporting to describe the strategic plans of the U.S. Air Force, but actually glorifying the militarists. The letter said:

"Re Anthony Leviero's 'Air War Across the Pole,' please do not fail to follow up your magnificent project for push-button bombing all the cities of the Soviet Union and North China from an atomic bomb station in Canada. I long to know how you propose to destroy the cities of South Africa, South America, India, the East and West Indies (not forgetting Ceylon and Madagascar) from a base in Antarctica. A third article might show that the remnants of the planet could be handed over to Franco, say, on Christmas Day, 1952."

Each step down the road of militarization heightens the hysteria; the demands of the services themselves become increasingly hysterical and no one thinks of putting forward a request for anything less than billions. How can anyone determine a "reasonable" figure for armaments or Marshall Plans when there is no set objective against which to measure the demand? "There is not now and has not been any integrated and co-ordinated postwar plan of defense," writes Hanson Baldwin. What is more, there is no single national policy into which an integrated military plan could fit — if there were an integrated military plan. There is nothing but the non-quantitative bombast of the Truman Doctrine: we must save our "way of life" at all cost, "and no matter what the cost, war would cost more." The whole thing degenerates into a pork-barrel scramble where the biggest brass, the fanciest gold-braid, and the most powerful bankers-turned-statesmen, imitate pigs at feeding time.

There is nothing in this setup, planless as it is (unless, indeed, there is a war plan, a time-table, that they conceal from us) to keep them from eating us out of house and home. For the Air Policy Commission's projected eighteen billions for arms in 1952 and the five or ten more per year required for "international affairs," are not the end of the matter. There is no end; the concealed strategic costs go on and on. Here are some:

Upward of two billions for a five- or six-year strategic stockpiling program; a National Science Foundation to aid military research at an eventual annual cost of over $120,-000,000; new armories and facilities for the expanded National Guard, $600,000,000; a half-billion goes to building new trans-sonic and supersonic wind tunnels; another half-billion for laboratories and proving grounds for new weapons and guided missiles. A series of such items causes Baldwin to raise the Air Policy Commission's purely military ante from eighteen to twenty-five billions.

But that's only the chicken-feed (or should I say swine-feed?) The generals and admirals are timid about asking for money, if you compare them with spokesmen for the biggest private interests. Take the oil companies. They have acquired vast foreign holdings largely at government expense, yielding profits largely tax-free, yet when they come forward—as they do now—with a plan for development of a synthetic fuel industry, they ask the government to assume the cost. The "civilian" Department of the Interior dutifully presents to the nation, with the approval of the Department of Defense (combined Army, Navy, Air Force), a proposal that the government initiate such a program at an eventual cost of — nine billion dollars!

And so on down the line. The payroll of our growing national and international spy systems ("intelligence") is another cost of the war orientation. The entire government outlay for civil aviation and the merchant marine (mail subsidies, harbor work, airport development) is for all practical purposes a military-strategic investment. We built a synthetic rubber industry in wartime and bear the cost of its maintenance in peacetime, as a military-strategic "necessity." And, as Baldwin observes, "each military capital investment entails a greater annual outlay for maintenance and depreciation."

What all this spells for civil liberties and the standard of living of the American people, it is not possible to demonstrate in a work of this kind. What we are concerned with here, is the impression our so-called "preparedness" makes on people abroad. Needless to say, the figures don't suggest peaceful intentions to them. Our "defense" plans and our Marshall Plan are seen in one framework. The whole behavior of the United States presents the threatening manners of a new military imperialism. Its range, as Baldwin described it in December, 1946, is global:

"The Army and Navy have agreed on a world-wide command set-up for the United States armed forces that provides unified command in the various theaters of operation from Germany and the Mediterranean to the Far East. . . . The Navy will be vested with command over all forces in a vast area of the Pacific from the Hawaiian Islands to and including the former Japanese-mandated islands.

"General Douglas MacArthur, who is Supreme Commander, Allied Forces, in Japan and Korea . . . will have operational command (in case of necessity) of the Bonins,

Volcanoes and Marianas, including the great naval bases at Guam . . . MacArthur also will command the Philippines and the Ryukyus, but United States Naval Forces in the Far East — the old Seventh Fleet — and the 10,000 Marines still remaining in China will be under the direct command of the Joint Chiefs of Staff.

"The agreements . . . provide for the establishment of a separate Alaskan command. . . . Other command agreements ... provide for the establishment of unified commands in the Caribbean under an Army officer, and of a northeast command for Newfoundland, Labrador and Greenland, also under an Army officer. The titles of the commanding officers in the European and Mediterranean Theaters may be changed slightly . . . but otherwise no great change . . . is involved."

Today you can stick a pin anywhere on the map and prick an American general or admiral. Yet by some miracle of smugness, this complete break with American tradition and assumption of military prerogatives beyond those ever claimed by any power in recorded history, is presented to the domestic audience as further proof of American generosity, disinterestedness, eagerness to serve others. Bosh! Who ever heard of admirals and generals absorbed in the moralities? Their business is to impose our foreign policy upon others by force if a show of force will not do the trick.

Our strategic expansion is not understandable without preliminary acknowledgment of other factors. These are, on the whole, rather widely known if not fully appreciated. First, we have attained worldwide air and naval and telecommunications supremacy in the course of two world wars. Supposedly non-military agreements covering American telecommunications, merchant shipping and civil-aviation privileges, are unmistakably strategic values. The three industries are universally recognized as basically military in character. They have been built, in every case, with the aid of government subsidies and for the avowed purpose of furthering the national interest or "national defense." Despite the insistence of the United States—to the point of fetishism—on "private enterprise" and "free competition" in every field, the United States Treasury footed the bill for American supremacy in these fields. Nor is the government stepping aside at this point to let the nominal owners run their industries as simple commercial undertakings. They remain United States government responsibilities because they are keys to world power.

Second, our general economic strength, based on the greatest productive plant in man's history, has given the United States an enormous though temporary advantage over all other industrial countries. One aspect of this economic margin over other powers is a sort of cosmopolitan technological superiority. We have a presumed monopoly of atomic explosives, for instance, despite the admitted lagging of American scientists in the field of atomic theory. General economic and technological leadership drew the necessary world-talent to a strictly American project, at a time when the United States alone was beyond the reach of bombers.

The overwhelming financial position of the United States is the decisive expression of its economic strength. The dependence of most of the world on American financial or economic "cooperation," provided the opportunity for the launching of the Marshall Plan. The Plan, in turn, would legalize and make permanent the dependence. Apologists for the plan assert the opposite. They say the plan is the very negation of imperialism because it tries to put the war-battered nations back on their own feet and end their dependence. But the official summary of the program says its terms would impose American limitations on the amount of factory-construction, power-plant establishment and even home-rebuilding, that any participant in the plan might undertake. Steel-mill construction and shipbuilding were particularly restricted. Thus it is clear the plan attempts to make our present advantages permanent by control of key portions of each country's economy. It therefore occasions no surprise to see only thinly veiled political controls following the economic ones.

There is an unreality about plans which contemplate "colonizing" the whole great, industrialized complex called Europe.* After all, it is not some superiority of the American character but the effects of war that make the temporary odds so great. The homes and factories of all Europe were damaged by the war; not one house in the United States was hit by an enemy shell or bomb, while our industry, stimulated by the war, expanded and retooled. A few years will cut down this war-created margin. Then what will happen to a policy built on the sand? At present, nevertheless, the odds are great and American policy rests upon them. Financial supremacy is the typical American instrument for the direct peacetime consolidation of our wartime gains. The political loan often indicates the full breadth of our strategic ambitions when military maps only hide the boundaries.

Against this background, the base-claims quietly staked out by the United States, acquire a new significance. Our aggressive foreign policy, our meaningful display of military, economic and financial power, contradict the casual tone in which our statesmen and publicists touch on the matter of American bases — when they touch on it at all. If we now collect all the claims in one pile, we shall indeed discover they are no trifling matter. They add up to a bid for absolute world domination. They also promise — if the American people do not intervene to drive the bankers and generals out of Washington — an ultimate resounding collapse of our foreign policy. Every inch of our present path is paved with the explosive materials of a new world war.

---

* Professor Hans Kohn, reviewing the first edition in the *Times* of June 13, quotes this passage and says I can rightly refer to such a plan as "unreal," for "certainly it is not the Marshall Plan." But very conservative writers—in the pages of the same paper—support me and contradict Prof. Kohn. See Chapter 15.

CHAPTER 4

CONQUEST OF POWER

American base-claims are not a startling break with an isolationist past. They did not emerge fully developed from the forehead of a suddenly power-crazed War or Navy Department. World War II was not the beginning of United States empire. Modern American imperialism is at least fifty years old and its roots, moreover, may be traced to earlier forms of expansion as old as our country. American expansion began in fact, almost as soon as the idea of independence took serious hold among colonial leaders.

I am not here suggesting that every form of growth of the original thirteen colonies was of an imperialist character. Indeed, I am not primarily concerned at this point with the character of our expansion at any time. I am interested only in rescuing an elementary truth from the grip of a national myth. The myth pretends that the United States was isolated and insulated from the world until the recent war — or at least until World War I. The truth is that the United States was plunged from — and by—its very birth into a long-term global struggle for power.

In its early stages, America's power-struggle was defensive but it was real and conscious. Several great world powers at first, and Great Britain all through America's history, sought by all means to restrict the growth and even the internal development of the United States. England blocked expansion where she could — both economic and territorial — and exploited political divisions within the country to check development. What more natural? In a capitalist world, relations among states are stamped by the sacred principle of unrestricted competition. Capitalist competition means, in practice, fierce struggle for domination of the world-market and the world itself. Each competitor tries to destroy all other competitors and thereby destroy competition. Each competing state strives for world domination.

Born into a world of fierce competion, the United States was subject to the laws of competition. The struggle for power that is implicit in such competition, put its stamp upon the very pattern of American economic development, a development that began with the desire for independence but soon discovered there is no independence — in such a world — short of supremacy. More and more the pattern of development sought, as its base, American supremacy on this continent as well as domination of adjacent islands. And more and more the direction of development was toward a level of strength which would permit a showdown with Great Britain. Nor, with Britain actively hindering America's development, could this process be wholly unconscious on either side. Britain, too, saw the danger, for from its birth the United States was recognized as enjoying the promise of ultimate growth to Great Power rank.

This is not hindsight. It may seem that no one could have previsioned the undeveloped American colonies of the 1770's, or the feeble independent United States of the 1780's and 1790's, as a Great Power. Still less, it would appear, could she have been recognized as potentially greater than the then ruling power of the world, Great Britain. But it is a fact that acute minds on both sides of the Atlantic saw that the revolted colonies had inherited what might easily prove decisive natural and historical advantages.

First, they had a vast hinterland for expansion, a whole continent to become the foundation of empire. Second, their continent lay between the two great oceans giving them an ultimate advantage in a seapower contest with Britain, whose home islands are so remote from the Pacific. Third, their relative isolation, in the state of communications then prevailing, promised a degree of immunity from European interference. At any rate, the British effort to inhibit United States expansion on the American continent would hardly succeed.

On both sides of the water, it was understood that the growth of American power and any eventual bid by the United States for world pre-eminence, would depend upon the development of American industry, to be followed by foreign trade and overseas expansion. Already in 1791, the House of Representatives asked for a report on how "to render the United States independent of foreign nations for military and other essential supplies." Secretary of the Treasury Alexander Hamilton made the report: "Not only the wealth but the independence and security of a country appear to be materially connected with the prosperity of manufactures." The whole course of the United States was thereafter more or less consciously charted toward industrial development on a continent-wide base.

Responsible statesmen *had* to forsee the power-potential of the weak American colonies. Without French aid, American independence could never have been achieved, yet when aid was sought, it was the duty of the dominant French Minister, Vergennes, to weigh the temporary advantage of hurting France's powerful enemy, Great Britain, against the permanent disadvantage if an American rival were thereby created. "We ask independence only for the thirteen states of America," he advised his King in 1778. "We do not desire that a new Republic shall arise which shall become the exclusive mistress of this immense continent."

In like manner, American statesmen had always to make immediate plans with a view to historical growth. The forms of American growth were dictated by America's weakness and Britain's strength. The United States had to seek territorial, industrial and commercial expansion where it was hardest for Britain to interfere, notably on the American continent. Another principle of American policy was to grow at the expense of European powers already weakened by Britain's rise. Thus, our early expansion was largely at the cost of Spain and France. A third principle dealt with timing. We expanded when Britain was too deeply engaged in European and Asiatic battles to pay attention to us. The American colonies won their independence in a global conflict—Britain against France, Holland, Spain and Russia for world empire—where we were about as important as, let us say, Burma in World War II. It is no accident that there were as many French as American troops at Yorktown when Cornwallis surrendered. American independence and United States expansion were functions of international relations from the very start, our national myth of isolation notwithstanding.

The ink was not dry in 1783 on the Treaty of Versailles, which settled the global issues along with the Anglo-American ones, when United States expansion began. As a matter of fact, plans for expansion preceded independence. The terms of the alliance with France in 1778 included the right of the United States to British possessions (other than the thirteen colonies themselves) which the new-born Republic might conquer in the course of the war. The Treaty of Versailles gave the United States all the territory between Canada and Florida east of the Mississippi. The United States immediately initiated a series of threats and forcible seizures that wrested Florida from declining Spain. Next, when Napoleon feared British seizure of French America and wished to strengthen Britain's American enemy, he offered us the Louisiana Territory for sixteen million dollars. Jefferson grabbed at this eagerly. It was part of the foreseen and foreseeable destiny of the land.

By the Louisiana Purchase we got the present states of Arkansas, Colorado, Iowa, Kansas, Louisiana, Minnesota, Missouri, Montana, Nebraska, North Dakota, Oklahoma, South Dakota and Wyoming. Various border settlements from Maine to Oregon, usually involving friction with England, filled out our territory to the North and Northwest while a series of intrigues and a war in the 1840's, plus the Gadsden Purchase in 1853, wrested from Mexico the present states of Texas, New Mexico, Colorado, Idaho, Utah, Nevada and California.

I am far from suggesting that this expansion was in itself evil, though the motives and methods sometimes were. If I were to make a "moral" judgment in this case, I would say that American continental expansion and the growth of the United States generally, up to perhaps 1880, fill a bright page in history. With all the seamy side of the record, the conquest of the continent marked an advance of the human race. It is not easy to forget the shameful treatment of the Indians, the thefts from the Mexicans, the brutal waste of human life in the development of the railroads and industries of the United States. Yet the early drive of America to expand, seems to me — on balance — primarily a drive to achieve a sufficiently strong physical basis to assure the national independence of the United States against all outside threats and pressures. The development of material resources here also spelled an increase in the whole world's powers of production. So far, therefore, we were on the side of the angels.

Yet I would wish to make this qualification: the compulsion to expansion that is inherent in capitalism, is the seed of future imperialism. The earliest American expansion contained within itself the dangerous drives characteristic of all imperialism. This inner drive for increased production, markets and profits, is bloody and brutal even in its pre-monopoy stages because it takes no thought for human values. The good and evil of capitalist expansion — the simultaneous development of material resources and crushing of the human being — are intermingled at every stage of America's growth as a world power. With the arrival of the great modern money power, the centralized, clique-ruled Morgan and Rockefeller "interest groups," new elements enter into the problem. But the basic principle that leads to the contemporary blustering Wall Street drive for world domination, was there waiting all the time: it is the capitalist principle of the primacy of things, the lawless rule of property over people.

If this element of latent danger is present even in the "natural" continental expansion of the United States—which has been compared to Czarist Russia's expansion into Siberia because both were true movements of settlers, intent on developing a sparsely-settled land—it is always more marked in our overseas expansion. Yet here we run into a sub-division of our national myth of isolation. The myth has it that American acquisitions overseas are largely the result of accident. The United States according to this pat theory, has never had any interest in acquiring colonies and to the extent that it did so, sheer blundering was responsible. The seizures from Spain at the turn of the century appear, in this theory, as the consequence of a temporary aberration, a "fit of imperialism" that passed quickly and never returned.

The record is to the contrary. For the past fifty years the United States has been expanding largely by other means than the open acquisition or annexation of territory. But even in the years before financial-industrial interests captured internal power and centered American policy on expansion abroad, there was a constant cumulation of positions that prepared our contemporary expansion. The Navy played the key role in this process. Traders, whalers, missionaries and shippers were free to go anywhere in pursuit of a dollar, and they had the right to protection by the Navy in their enterprises. The Navy, in turn constituted itself a kind of super-Department of State. Together with the overseas commercial interests, it built up an unofficial empire, or got semi-official footholds, which awaited only the right international circumstances to get formal recognition at home.

Charles Oscar Paullin's *Diplomatic Negotiations of American Naval Officers*, written by a worshipper of the

Navy, describes this process of building an empire behind the back of the people. Paullin tells how the "sailor-diplomat," set up American *de facto* dependencies in all parts of the world. There was Master-Commandant Thomas Ap Catesby Jones who forced upon Hawaii, in 1826, the first treaty that country ever signed with a foreign power, though not until 1898 did the United States openly proclaim its possession of the islands. There was Commander Richard A. Meade who in December, 1871, signed a treaty with Pago Pago's great chief, Mauga Maimoi, giving the United States dominance and a naval station. This unauthorized treaty, angrily opposed by the Germans, was not ratified by the Senate, yet Paullin is certainly correct in saying that "to the decisive action of Meade the United States owes its present colonial possession in Samoa." On every continent and on every sea, the naval "diplomat" made a constant "display of concrete force" and lined up claims that could be turned into possessions when the proper moment in national politics arrived or the international situation was favorable.

This history of American overseas expansion culminates at two points: 1898-1905, and 1939-1946. The development of American capitalism was far enough advanced by 1898 to bring the United States into the great imperialist space-grab taking place at that time. But the annexations of the next few years were merely the consummation of years of penetration. Apologists for present-day American expansionism cannot pretend mere ignorance when they treat our acquisitions of 1898-1905 as seizures without past preparation. (All the less can they do this, as I shall show later, in connection with our 1939-1946 gains).

Charles A. Beard is emphatic about this point in his, *The Idea of the National Interest.* Discussing the seizure of the Philippines, for instance, he says:

"A long series of commercial and naval efforts, deliberately conceived in terms of interest and far from accidental in character, had produced a desired result. If such things are 'accidents,' then politics and statecraft are meaningless frivolities. If these are 'accidents' what are deliberate determinations of policy?"

Beard further suggests that only a broad program of expansion could explain the war with Spain since "documents now available" show that our supposed objective, the independence of Cuba, "could have been obtained by diplomatic pressure on Spain." But this would not have given us what we obtained by going to war: "a naval base at Guantanamo (Cuba), commanding the Windward Passage; nor would it have furnished the occasion for annexing Puerto Rico, commanding the Mona Passage, or for acquiring the Philippines, which supplied a naval base for commercial expansion in the Orient."

To deny the obvious significance of this pattern just because "no such comprehensive policy of expansion" was publicly revealed, would be to ignore the universal practice of concealing harsh truths about self-interest until at least twenty years after the event. Nevertheless, says Beard, "the conformity of the outcome to the pattern of commercial and naval expansion could not have been neater had it been deliberately planned. Nor could it be accurately described as a historic accident, as was once the fashion; for it was the perfect upshot of a long chain of actions and leadership extending back over more than half a century."

Against our present background of a century and a half of expansion, it is easier to see how statesmen and students of public affairs long ago predicted America's great role in the world. They could not foresee the details, but they could name the main forces.

The development of American industry, the flow of European capital to the United States, the unlimited resources of the continent and its relative isolation, promised to add up to eventual Great Power status and a challenge for world rule. Already in 1841, the German economist,

Friederich List, could say as much in his *National System of Political Economy*:

"The same causes to which England owes her present elevation, are very likely to bring America, in the course of the coming century, to a degree of industry, wealth and power that will place it as far above England as England is above Holland today."

Forty years later, Britain's noted statesman, Gladstone, added a postscript: "It is she alone who, at a coming time, can and probably will wrest from us our commercial supremacy. We have no title: I have no inclination to murmur at this prospect. If she acquires it, she will make the requisition by the right of the strongest and best. We have no more title against her than Venice or Genoa or Holland has had against us."

Forty more years elapse and World War I sends the United States skyrocketing to first place in world economy and world finance. In his *America Conquers Britain* (1930), Ludwell Denny quoted an "enthusiastic American banker" as saying the United States had now fulfilled the prediction. Gloated the banker: "No other nation ever before was at one and the same time the world's greatest producer of goods, exporter, reservoir of capital, and dispenser of credit; our place is one of dominant power." Denny thought the claim premature but was sure we were "headed in that direction—despite British competition."

A few years later, 1940, World War II had begun and the United States was giving Britain slowly increasing aid. It was headed toward full participation in the war—at a price to Great Britain. The price was—British surrender of strategic domination of the globe, final acknowledgement of American world supremacy. John MacCormac says exactly that in the very title of his 1940 book, *America and World Mastery*. He wrote:

"Every day makes it more certain that the United States must not only put herself at the head of the English-speaking people to win this war of which a free world is the prize but that, after having won the world, the United States must be prepared to run it. Therefore, to the extent that England grows weak the United States must grow strong. As England's grasp on world power shrinks, American dominion must expand, and where England's dominance ends American coercion must begin."

That would apear to describe what has actually happened. It was Britain's announced decision to withdraw from the job of policing Greece, it will be recalled, that precipitated the proclamation of the Truman Doctrine. "American coercion" has replaced British coercion in Greece and elsewhere. More and more Britain is reduced to an utterly second-rate position, to the role of a mere tributary of the United States, as Holland, Belgium, Portugal and their empires were tributary to Britain for so many decades.

By a policy of capitulation, the Labor Government hastens this process and when it meets domestic criticism, it cries:

"Many of us expect Britain to act as if she were still, as in the nineteenth century, the only world power in existence, a mighty empire unchallenged either in the military or economic sphere." This is from a pamphlet issued by the Labor Party in May 1947 which complained that America "has undisputed control of half the earth and all the oceans."

Our power is not so absolute as Mr. Bevin's apologists would have it, but there is no doubt that the United States has displaced Britain as the leading capitalist state and imperial power. And from that eminence the United States, secure in the smug official estimate of our own high morality, is now demanding world rule in the name of "world leadership."

CHAPTER 5

A HEMISPHERE FOR ONE

American plans for expansion were not limited to the North American continent even at the outset. From the day of independence, the United States not only marked out the continent as its own, but looked to the hemisphere as its broader base of power and the Pacific as its principal field for overseas expansion. Even this advance planning had to be done in terms of military-strategic power, for if we wanted a sphere of influence we would have to take it away from someone else. The world was already fully divided, if not politically — that was to come later, from 1870 to 1900 — then economically and strategically. British arms ruled the globe. American thinking was therefore always in terms of strategic expansion more than immediate economic advantages. Moreover, this emphasis on power rather than direct profit, suited the American situation in another respect. Unlike Britain, we had a huge continent providing such rich resources and so big a market that for a century there was no violent compulsion to seek immediate benefit of major overseas economic outlets. Early expansion was rather in terms of ultimate need, in terms of the foreseeable day when American industry should have grown so great on the continent, fattened so much on its huge home market, that it would have to expand or burst. American capitalism would then need the hemisphere and the Pacific as secure markets and fields of investment.

Alexander Hamilton urged the earliest effort to earmark the hemisphere for American future use. He predicted the United States would organize the two continents into a "great American system, superior to the control of all trans-Atlantic force or influence and able to dictate the terms of connection between the Old and the New World."

In the 1820's, we declined to join Britain in a statement barring intervention by the Holy Alliance against the revolted South American republics. Instead, we laid down the Monroe Doctrine unilaterally, at least partly for the reason that we wanted eventually to say, "Keep out," to Britain as well as the others. In short, we began to stake out our claim to ultimate sole domination of the hemisphere.

The Caribbean was our starting point. The Caribbean is not only the strategic key to hemisphere control, but by its domination of the narrows between the two continents it governs the traffic between the Atlantic and the Pacific. "One thing is sure — in the Caribbean Sea is the strategical key to two great oceans, the Atlantic and the Pacific; our own chief maritime frontiers," wrote Admiral Mahan, whose theories have had a powerful influence on American foreign policy.

Struggle for a foothold in the Caribbean began before independence. American colonists defied the British ban on colonial trade with the West Indies. Large-scale smuggling, flourishing in an atmosphere of patriotic indignation with British monopoly practices, contributed to the development of the New England shipping and fishing industries. By the 1820's, we had already put in a claim to control of Cuba and were looking forward to an expansion of influence and power through the cutting of a Panamanian or Nicaraguan canal. We attained the strength to demand parity with Britain in any such enterprise — or reluctantly to concede British parity — by 1850, when the Clayton-Bulwer Treaty specified that the canal should be "neutral." But in the 1880's we suddenly announced that we would run the future canal alone; that an out-dated treaty could not govern us in time of war, that we would not admit British parity in the Caribbean. By 1895, when we stepped into a dispute between British Guiana and Venezuela, over a claim to thirty thousand square miles of jungle, we asserted absolute American supremacy, not over the Caribbean alone but over the entire hemisphere.

"Today the United States is practically sovereign on this continent, and its fiat is law," Secretary of State Olney cockily informed Great Britain, herself no stranger to imperialist arrogance. "Its infinite resources combined with its isolated position render it master of the situation and practically invulnerable against any or all other powers."

This was somewhat premature. The British had an extensive system of bases in the hemisphere and particularly in the Caribbean; we had none. A war between us would have found Britain with all the early advantages. In the long haul, however, the factors cited by Olney would have been decisive and, in any event, there was no question which way the United States was moving. It would take a "local" war and two world wars to settle the issue, but how it would be settled was written on the wall.

By the war of 1898, which has been called "an imperialist war if ever there was one," we took away from feeble Spain her Caribbean possessions. She ceded Puerto Rico, a first-rate strategic asset. The real relations of power, however, radically affected territories never formally annexed by the United States. American rule and complete American strategic domination of Cuba, Haiti, the Dominican Republic, and Nicaragua resulted. American military occupation of Cuba, declared "independent" of Spain in 1898, lasted until we had reduced the country to permanent subordination and acquired the Guantanamo base we still hold. Next we forced Colombia to recognize the "independence" of Panama where we carved out a canal zone and put it under direct American rule. In fact the Panama Republic itself is hardly less American-ruled than is Puerto Rico; Cuba, than Alaska. The forms are different, that is all. This is conceded by all serious commentators. A semi-governmental committee under the direction of Thomas W. Lamont, late head of the Morgan banking system, provides a supporting view in a 1933 study called, *American Financial Foreign Policy*. The report listed all these Caribbean lands and said:

"All of the countries are indisputably within the sphere of special influence of the United States, financial as well as political, even though the influence is in some cases overtly manifested only at intervals."

Banker Lamont's study does not pretend that our respect for the "independence" of such states is more than nominal. "Our investments in the Caribbean as a whole amount to some $2,867,000,000," it notes, adding: "A stake of that size, in practice if not in theory, apparently justifies some disregard for the refinements of constitutionality."

Even without frank violations of the constitutions of many weaker states, financial "influence" amounts in many cases to powerful control. In May 1947 the President of Haiti revealed that his regime's immediate program was to pay off a $6,000,000 debt to American bondholders in order to "liberate" his country. Elected in August, 1946, President Dumarsais Estime said he found Haiti's hands tied because her customs receipts are collected under American supervision, for payment of interest to the bondholders, in a manner leaving nothing for Haiti. Nor would the United States lend him money to get rid of interest obligations all out of line with present cheap money rates.

"Every time we asked the United States to remove its financial control, we were told that we first must pay the pending bonds. We therefore asked for $20,000,000 to take care of the bonds and get rid of paying their high interest of six per cent and have something left for public works and agricultural development. But we were turned down."

It is worth re-emphasizing that power factors were uppermost in bringing about American expansion in the Caribbean. The Lamont-supervised report asserts that "these territorial acquisitions were not effected in even minor degree for the purpose of protecting or consolidating previously existing American economic interests in the regions affected. . . . *What was involved was* the protection of our Latin American commitments as a whole, and the preservation of opportunities for further commercial and financial expansion, *not primarily a desire to exploit* the economic possibilities of *the specific regions themselves.*" In short, *the strategic value of the Caribbean for* its ultimate prize of *"commercial and financial expansion" on a world scale,* was what the United States had in mind. Lamont might be inclined, of course, to minimize the specific gains of private interests, as a kind of whitewash of financial imperialism. But this sort of analysis cannot be dismissed as whitewash; it is, in fact, a damaging admission of the most ambitious kind of imperialism: the drive for world power.

New economic and political positions captured by the United States during and as a result of World War I, registered hardly any change in America's open holdings of territory and power. We acquired the Virgin Islands from Denmark by purchase in 1917. After the war, in the 1920's, America "overtly manifested" its rule of the Caribbean by the use of troops. Military expeditions forcibly imposed American ideals and "protected" American interests in Nicaragua, Haiti, the Dominican Republic and other countries, while various forms of "dollar diplomacy" backed up our arms in Cuba and Middle America* generally. There is no doubt that American dominance of the Caribbean and a wide extension of American influence in Middle and South America had been achieved by this time. So long, however, as the British had Canada and an imposing array of bases in the hemisphere, American supremacy was not a fact.

---

* It is convenient to divide the Hemisphere into North America (U. S., Canada, etc.) Middle America (Mexico, Central America, West Indies) and South America. From the point of view of strategy and power this is also more realistic than the familiar North, Central and South America.

World War II fixed that. At the very outbreak of the war, Great Britain surrendered all her bases in the Western Hemisphere as the price of American aid and of our ultimate direct participation in the war. The tail goes with the hide: by the British base-transfer, American supremacy in North and South America, specifically including Canada, was fully conceded. Here again, John MacCormac calls a spade a spade and not a shovel. Noting that bases on Newfoundland, the Bermudas, the Bahamas, Jamaica, Antigua, St. Lucia, Trinidad and British Guiana had been acquired within six months of the war's outbreak, culminating more than a century of American pressure to drive European influence out of the New World, he remarked cheerfully:

"The United States, by means of Lease-Lend aid, is already buying on installments the kind of postwar world it wants. If 'imperialism' is 'the extension of the control, dominion or empire of a nation'—and that is how Webster defines it—the United States has been practicing it on a very respectable scale since this war began . . . During no previous period of her history has the United States ever achieved so wide an extension of her dominion and power in so short a time."

What had she achieved? She had apparently achieved full, unchallenged military-strategic control of the Hemisphere. She had added to the American Empire, all of North, South and Middle America—if not from the North Pole to the South Pole, at least from the North Pole to Argentina or the Falkland Islands. The whole of Canada, Newfoundland, Labrador and the territories stretching toward the Arctic Sea, Alaska and the Bering Straits had for all practical purposes been surrendered by Great Britain to the United States. The ultimate resistance of the American nations to *all* imperialisms, may greatly modify this estimate. But that is another story, another chapter; perhaps it will be the final chapter in the history of imperialism. Here we are dealing only with the position as between two great imperialist rivals. And in the record of the centuries-long struggle of American imperialism to overtake and displace the British as the foremost capitalist power in all the world, MacCormac's estimate appears justified. He exults:

"In acquiring an air base, a naval base and a site for a military defense force on Newfoundland, the United States has obtained a strategic position which effectively, completely and permanently, 'contains' Canada. For Canada is a long bottle of which the St. Lawrence River is the neck, and Newfoundland is the cork in the neck of that bottle. . . . In securing a base on Newfoundland, the United States not only secured a potential stranglehold on Canada but a substantial extension of its power and domination in the northern half of the Western Hemisphere . . . The United States is in virtual possession of a whole continent and in control of a whole hemisphere."

What acquisition of the Newfoundland base meant for domination of Canada, a chain of bases, airfields and special rights accomplished for the rest of the hemisphere. Especially since we already had all the other strategic aces —Panama, Cuba, Puerto Rico. Britain still retains formal possession of certain territories in the hemisphere but that gives her only the expense and irritation of administering them. The power and the profit have passed to the United States.

The current policy of welding the hemisphere into one military system employing uniform American equipment, building bases to American specifications, using American military instructors, and accepting common commitments in the event of a future war, rounds out the picture. So far as Canada is concerned, the tight wartime "coordination" of military activity with the United States and under United States control, was extended indefinitely into peacetime by an unprecedented agreement in February, 1947.

One member of Canada's parliament went so far as to say: "This could easily be the Munich of 1947."

The last link in the hemisphere chain was completed when General Marshall broke a long deadlock in the State Department in May 1947, committing the United States to supply arms to Latin American governments. President Truman thereupon asked Congress to pass enabling legislation which would permit the United States to "train soldiers, sailors and airmen" from the Arctic to the Antarctic, in "a program of military collaboration" which would make United States methods, organization and equipment the standard for the entire hemisphere.

By supplying American arms and standardizing Latin American equipment, the Army-Navy men expect to tie every government south of the border to Washington's apron strings. The move prepares the way for absorption of Argentina, last holdout of the hemisphere, into the American sphere of influence. Thus the whole range of American policies and acquisitions adds up to proposed conversion of the hemisphere into a single gigantic armed base for military operations of the future. It is a base of proportions beyond anything history has heretofore seen.

CHAPTER 6

AN AMERICAN LAKE

Mastery of the hemisphere cannot, in the nature of the endlessly expanding competitive principle on which capitalism works, mark a final limit to American ambition. On the contrary, defense of "our" continent and expansion of our world claims, lead to establishment of bases far out in the two oceans, thousands of miles from the American continent. Bases far from the American continent must be defended in turn. That calls for bases on the continents at the opposite side of the oceans. Inevitably, the logic of "defense" by domination, leads to struggle for a world-wide strategic system under the American flag. "The strategic defenses of the United States are not at the three-mile limit in American waters, but extend across both oceans and to all the trans-oceanic lands from which an attack by sea or by air can be launched," says Walter Lippman. The nature of modern communications, requiring round-the-world relay stations; the tremendous development of aviation, resting on world-wide air facilities; the still critical role of navies and their merchant auxiliaries in intercontinental warfare such as we have just experienced, reinforce this urge to spread out from our huge hemispheric base until our "defenses" have become a global system menacing the security of all other nations.

As a matter of fact, our overseas expansion has always been conditioned on realization that we must someday become what now we are — the giant who claims rule of the Western double-continent. And so, from the beginning, the American Republic sought that larger political-economic-strategic "freedom" which the future United States would require. This ambition — before it reached its present form suspiciously like the lebensraum concept — was rather automatically directed toward the Pacific.

"The United States, from the very beginning, shared in European expansion to the East," wrote Professor George Taylor in his *America in the New Pacific.* She "began her Far Eastern career when she was a small and not very powerful country, long before she became a continental power, before the Panama Canal had been built, before tin and rubber became important raw materials for national defense, before there were heavy American investments in the East."

It was not just a "share" in expansion, however, that the United States sought. It was absolute control of the Pacific. "An ambition to win mastery of the Pacific and control its rich commerce runs persistently through the entire history of the United States," says Foster Rhea Dulles, in *America in the Pacific.* "It was a powerful motivating force in every acquisition of territory on the Pacific from Oregon and California to Hawaii and the Philippines. This is not to say that these instances of territorial growth can be neatly fitted into exactly the same pattern, but there is a thread of consistency in this expansion which draws our possessions together as component parts of a Pacific Empire."

Why did the United States turn automatically toward the Pacific for fulfillment of empire ambitions? It did so because there Britain could least effectively employ her great power to stifle American competition. There the United States could most effectively employ its limited power. Britain, after all, was located in the distant Atlantic. Thus the great conscious formulators of the Pacific Empire dream, men like William Seward and Commodore Matthew Calbraith Perry, saw the matter.

"They recognized England as the United States' most dangerous rival and felt that in the Western Ocean lay our best opportunity for effective competition against British trade and political power," says Dulles.

Trade, of course, meant trade with Asia, the profits of

commerce with China, the carrying trade, business in every country on the vast continent across the sea. Even our continental expansion was sometimes a result rather than a cause of our larger overseas ambitions. Dulles assembles evidence that we spread to the Pacific Coast more out of interest in China than out of interest in the coastal lands themselves.

"The expansionists of [President Polk's] day seldom dwelt upon what Oregon or California might mean to the United States," he says. The great debate raged over their value in enabling us to "command the commerce of the east." The first American settlement on the coast, in 1811, "forerunner to the occupation of both Oregon and California," was Astoria. And Astoria was established by John Jacob Astor for trade with Asia. As he wrote later to John Quincy Adams, he wished to set up a depot for Columbia River furs because he desired to conduct "a trade across the continent to that river, and from thence to Canton, in China," and on around the globe to the United States, of which the West was as yet no part.

This early trade with Canton, only port of Imperial China open to foreigners, was richly rewarding. An American vessel of less than a hundred tons carrying a $9,000 cargo, made $60,000 on a single trip; a larger ship obtained $284,000 on a $50,000 risk. But effective competition with Great Britain for these plums was possible only if there were power to back up our competing claims at the time and places of conflict. So while merchants, missionaries, capitalists, whalers and traders competed with their opposite British numbers for private advantage in all parts of the Pacific, naval officers and diplomats — themselves often from the ranks of business — persistently pressed American claims to sole American possession of islands and ports having strategic value.

During the War of 1812, Captain David Porter beached his frigate "Essex" on Nukuhiva Island, one of the Washington group in the Marquesas, renamed it Madison Island and "annexed" it for the United States. Nothing came of his flag-raising on November 19, 1813, or his proclamation, prophetic of future imperialist "moral" hokum, that the "natives . . . have requested to be admitted into the great American family whose pure Republican policy approaches so near their own." But it started the long series of claims that laid a basis for ultimate American control of hundreds of such bases.

The series is continuous. The United States established a Pacific station in 1821; a "treaty" was signed with Hawaii in 1826; our future base at Pago Pago in the island of Tutuila, Samoas, was first visited by Commodore Charles Wilkes in 1839; in 1844, two years after the British forced China open to unlimited British trade, the United States imposed a like treaty for America; in 1846, John Quincy Adams was certain that "the spirit of aggrandizement" had seized on the American people and would forever after "characterize their history."

By mid-century we were in the thick of a battle with Britain for Pacific supremacy, a battle whose course was prolonged and decision postponed by the domestic conflict that culminated in the Civil War. Yet the nature of the decision was no secret. Matthew Calbraith Perry, blasting Japan open to trade in 1853, said the United States was forced to do it in order "to anticipate the designs of that unconscionable government, the British, whose cupidity was limited only by its capacity to satisfy it."

Perry, younger brother of the hero of the battle of Lake Erie, was urging various annexations even before he reached Japan. "The course of coming events will ere long make it necessary for the United States to extend its jurisdiction beyond the limits of the Western continent, and I assume the responsibility of urging the expediency of establishing a foothold in this quarter of the globe," Perry wrote.

He suggested seizure of what he called the Loo Choo

Islands (now the Japanese Ryukyus, which are urged as permanent United States bases by many naval bigwigs). In May 1853, Perry put into Napa in the Loo Choos where he came to agreement with the Regent for use of Napa as his squadron base. At Port Lloyd (later, under the Japanese, known as Ogasawara Jima) on Peel Island in the Bonins, he raised the American flag. He urged that he be ordered to seize the Bonins to set up firm bases for controlling the trade with Japan. Perry also visited Formosa and suggested a protectorate there. Dr. Peter Parker, our commissioner in China in 1856, followed this up by proposing a deal with the French and British by which we would get Formosa. Two American traders, established on that island and holding a monopoly of the export trade, even raised the American flag over their little settlement.

The time was not ripe for such acquisitions, but today the precedents are used to back American claims to strategic positions in every one of these islands, whether now owned by Japan as in the case of the Ryukyus and Bonins, or by China, as in the case of Formosa.

Acquisition of Alaska, with its Aleutian Islands, may also be considered primarily in the light of American expansion into the Pacific rather than as a part of continental development. Russia offered Alaska to the United States in 1867, and Seward, out of firm faith in his vision of American rule in the Pacific, overcame a great deal of opposition and swallowed lots of ridicule to buy it. The United States also acquired a few minor islands such as Midway in 1859 and part of the Samoas in deals with Britain and Germany —at the expense of the native inhabitants—in the 1870's and 1880's.

Though Hawaii was not formally annexed until 1898, it was also firmly lodged in our power-system long before that. American missionaries and traders, with indirect government aid, defeated their British rivals, capturing the best native land and souls for "our side." As early as 1853, the

Hawaiian government, firmly controlled by American interests, vainly petitioned for annexation. (Though it must be admitted that the American sugar planters were more loyal to their own pocketbooks than to any ideal of American expansion; when the McKinley Act later denied them certain favors they sought — because mainland interests were opposed—they were ready to turn the islands over to Britain or Canada.) In 1875, however, a treaty "pledging the Hawaiian government not to alienate any port or territory in the kingdom to any other power, virtually made Hawaii an economic colony," according to Julius W. Pratt, whose *Expansionists of 1898* is an authoritative study. A new treaty in 1887 gave the United States exclusive use of Pearl Harbor as a coaling and repair station. Of any of these acts, therefore, it would have been proper to observe, as Walter Lippmann did later in connection with formal annexation:

"By this action the Western defenses of the United States were thrust out into a great circle from Kiska in the Aleutians through Midway Island to Samoa. From San Francisco as a center the radius of that circle runs over 3,000 miles out into the Pacific."

Yet in the Pacific, as in the Caribbean, true empire had to wait on war. The "local" war of 1898, provoked by the United States and fought in two naval theaters separated by thousands of miles of land and water, put us into the Pacific with a splash. The Philippine Islands were ceded by Spain and their inhabitants subdued by force. Under cover of the war, we also completed the annexation of Hawaii. Such strategic islands as Guam were added to our holdings. Only a handful of Americans, even among the intelligentsia, today understand what these acquisitions meant in terms of power, in terms of the sphere of influence forecast by their seizure. Writing in 1943, Walter Lippman said of the annexation of the Philippines:

"This committed the United States to the defense of a large territory nearly 7,000 nautical miles west of California, but only 700 miles off the China Coast, only 250 miles from Formosa, only 1,700 miles from Yokohama, and less than 1,400 miles from Singapore. A circle which has Manila as its center, and a radius of about 1,500 miles, encloses the industrial region of Japan, all of Korea, practically all of China proper, French Indo-China, British Burma and Malaya, and the Netherlands Indies. Thus by the acquisition of the Philippines, the United States had placed itself at the geographical center of the empires of Eastern Asia, and at the strategic center of their lines of communication."

If acquisition of the Philippines staked out our claim to so vast an empire as far back as 1898, what shall we say today of the extent of American ambitions? No part of the Pacific is exempt from our demand for hegemony. At the Southwest end of the Pacific Theater, our troops in Australia and New Zealand a year after the war ended were a reminder that those countries are themselves land anchors of our Pacific Empire. Our demands for unilateral control of defense systems in their own part of the world — demands that have moved these countries to seek a joint counter-defense system together with Great Britain— would push Australia and New Zealand into the role of American dependencies. The "joint" defense system we propose to share with Great Britain, Australia and New Zealand — given our present troop positions and possessions, our overwhelming industrial, arms-making, naval, aviation, military and financial power — would place us on top even if we planned a partnership.

But in truth the United States has no thought of starting an equal partnership. We are asking the British, Australians and New Zealanders to surrender to the United States the sovereignty of certain islands; we are claiming Pacific hegemony and are backing our claims with bases presently in our possession; we have troops on the ground, ships on the scene, planes overhead, financial pressure in the background. We are not discussing; we are telling them.

Under these conditions, negotiations concerning twenty-five Pacific Islands belonging to Great Britain and New Zealand began in Washington in March 1946 and were apparently uncompleted at the end of 1947. The islands lie in a 2,150-mile area east of New Guinea and south of the Marshall and Hawaiian Islands. They are not to be confused with the former Japanese mandates. British mandated islands over which the United States reportedly asked nothing less than American flag sovereignty, include Nukufetau, Funafuti, Nukulaelae, Carondelet Reef, Sydney, Hull, Gardner, McKean, Christmas, Flint, Birnie, Phoenix, Enderbury, Canton, Starbuck, Malden, Caroline, Vostock islands. Canton and Enderbury are included despite the fact that the United States and Great Britain agreed to a 50-year co-dominion as late as 1939. The American attitude is, "Yes, but that was 1939." New Zealand mandates reportedly demanded include Atafu, Nakunono, Danger, Rakahanga, Manihiki, Tongareva.

It was plainly stated that these negotiations were but a step in "a vast program of securing U. S. bases" and that next steps would point toward Australian mandates and French Pacific possessions. Encroachments on British Oceania (the Fijis, Tonga, Solomons) have not been fully defined but American strategic claims on the Solomons have been most frequently mentioned. With respect to Australia, a huge American-built base on Manus in the Admiralty Islands, is the central issue. There is no demand for American withdrawal. Australia asks only to share in the operation of the base, and Britain and New Zealand propose that Manus have a place in a Southwest Pacific defense scheme they are considering. American authorities testily reply that we built Manus, we will have to maintain it, the burden of a war would fall on us anyway, so we want to operate it without "interference" by the nation that happens to have sovereignty over the territory. This deadlock was long unresolved, but the United States could afford delay: it remained in sole possession of Manus.

The six hundred and twenty-three former Japanese mandated islands, along with the non-mandates, for all practical purposes become United States possessions. Together with the Philippines and the Hawaiian Islands, they fit into the United States flag system which is to form the central strategic pattern of the Pacific. Around this system supporting systems are contemplated. British Empire states would operate part of these secondary systems and parts may be under nominal United Nations trusteeship. But it should not be imagined that these minor territories, by operating under United Nations authority, will escape the same full integration into American strategic plans as territories under our own flag. It is specifically intended that territories and populations in the trusteeships shall become a part of the ruling power's military apparatus.

Sydney Gruson, reporting to the *New York Times* from London on June 24, 1946, noted that proposed African trusteeship agreements approved by Britain, France, Belgium and South Africa, contain "a significant departure from the mandate agreements drawn up after the first World War. The administering authority would be entitled to establish naval, military and air bases in the territory, to fortify it and to mobilize its manpower and resources for the maintenance of international peace and security. Under the mandates, the administering authority could raise troops only for local defense and could not militarize the territory." The United States, in submitting its own formula for American trusteeship of various Pacific islands later, went further than the Franco-British group. It demanded that American power in the islands be as full as it is where the United States rules without benefit of the

United Nations. These military demands of the powers were incorporated in the agreements finally approved by a UN majority and put into effect by the Trusteeship Council despite Soviet denunciation of the procedure as "illegal."

By all these means, the United States has gained full possession of island territories assuring her of sole strategic command of the Pacific. The Pacific Ocean has become an American lake, alike for commerce or for any war the United States may wage across the sea. No pious formula can reconcile this reality with our pretense that "we seek no territorial aggrandizement." No, not even Senator Vandenberg's self-righteous boast: "We do not like 'expansionism' by anybody in a new world which is pledged to the humanities of the Atlantic Charter."

CHAPTER 7

THE GEM OF ALL OCEANS

The great hemisphere power-base dominated by the United States, leads automatically to American claims for sole mastery of the two oceans. Britannia used to rule the waves, and there are still people both in the United Kingdom and the United States who can't realize that this is no longer true. A look at the shipping figures, showing America with more than half the whole world's war and merchant tonnage, is enough to establish the real state of affairs. And no matter what the peacetime level the United States may set for its Navy and merchant marine, everyone now clearly understands that quantitative superiority can be reasserted at short notice. It is a common boast in certain American circles that the Atlantic Ocean is just as much an American lake as the Pacific. In his retirement report, Admiral Nimitz stated flatly that the United States now has a control of the sea "more absolute than was possessed by the British" at the peak of their power.

Nor is this an empty boast or a mere boast. On the contrary, the British government says as much. In a quasi-governmental pamphlet defending the policies of Foreign Minister Ernest Bevin, issued in May 1947, the Labor Party ascribed many British difficulties to this shift in seapower. It flatly asserted United States hegemony in the Atlantic no less than the Pacific Ocean.

It is so simple an admission that its breathtaking implications may easily be missed. In a world whose domination was contested by Great Britain and the United States, mastery of the Atlantic was mastery of the world. The outline of American expansion in the Atlantic itself is rather clear. We have Greenland, and only babes in the wood think it will ever be given back to Denmark or released from American strategic domination. We have Newfoundland and Labrador. In Iceland and the Azores, negotiations have gone on while our troops remained in the key places; history shows such negotiations leave their mark. Indeed, in all the uproar about Soviet negotiations with Iran shortly after the war ended, British and American representatives made all points applicable to our own case: we may say without hesitation that Iceland and the Azores will continue in the American strategic system along with such war-acquired rights as we have in Britain's Ascension Island.

Ascension isn't just Ascension. It is a symbol of the far reach of our base system in the Atlantic. The Army Air Forces publicly boast of "a chain of air bases stretching from the Azores to the Arctic Circle," operated by the Atlantic Division of the Air Transport Command, with authority over all ground forces in the division. "This vast network of bases covering 26,492,750 square miles of ocean," says a dispatch obviously inspired by the AAF, "included Fort Pepperil, Newfoundland; Goose Bay, Labrador; Narsarssuak, Greenland; Meeks Field, Iceland; Harmon Field, Newfoundland; Kindley Field, Bermuda; Santa Maria, Azores; Natal, Brazil; and Ascension." Other parts of the network are thirty or forty ATC standby fields and weather observation posts in Greenland, Iceland and Canada.

The Navy, including the naval air force, being as separate and jealous a power system as any foreign nation, we should have to enumerate its bases in the same fashion, if it were our purpose to have an account complete in every detail rather than an overall picture. But a list of bases, however long, will not provide even a preliminary sketch for the overall picture of the United States in the Atlantic.

To understand it, we must again refer to the whole history of the American struggle to overthrow British world rule. The United States at first expanded where it could avoid direct conflict with Britain, but the growth of

American empire brought many clashes with British sea-power in the Atlantic, the area of Britain's most jealous domination.

The preliminary skirmishes of the Atlantic began the day the United States was born. The name of the battle was — "freedom of the seas." Our school textbooks present the American struggle for freedom of the seas as the purest kind of morality. Diplomats and publicists follow the same easy pattern. But in truth, the putting forward of the issue is but a tactic. John MacCormac notes that it was our weapon against Britain when Britain ruled the waves, because it "is a policy for weak trading nations." Professor Williams, in his *Economic Foreign Policy of the United States*, likewise mocks the customary treatment of America's battle for freedom of the seas. He quotes with scorn the assertion of John Bassett Moore that we plugged for freedom of the seas out of pure doctrinaire devotion to the Declaration of Independence. All through the struggle, the conventional historian Moore orates, "the keynote was freedom; freedom of the individual, in order that he might work out his destiny in his own way; freedom in government, in order that the human faculties might have free course; freedom in commerce, in order that the resources of the earth might be developed and rendered fruitful in the increase of human wealth, contentment and happiness."

By an obvious effort of the will, Professor Williams avoids dismissing this effort with an unscholarly, "Nuts." He comments: "This statement attributes to our forefathers a philanthropy and idealism in their commercial policy which is more than human . . . [Their] purpose was based upon the immediate desire to provide trade for American ships and to sell such products as fish, lumber, and farm products rather than upon the humanitarian motive of developing the resources of the world for the increase of human contentment. The wealth, contentment, and happiness of British shipowners, for example, was of no concern to the United States."

Certainly not. The wealth and happiness of British shipowners were due to British world dominance, near-monopoly of manufacturing and commerce, to the detriment of America. British restrictive laws, backed by British naval supremacy, limited American participation in foreign trade. This had a depressing effect on American industry. So of course America was for freedom of the seas. Without it, merchants and shipowners could not make profits; domestic industries, insofar as they depended directly or indirectly on shipping and commerce, were cramped and starved. In sum, the wellbeing of the whole nation was affected.

Economic grievances were not the only injuries cited in the Declaration of Independence. Liberty in general and freedom of the seas were real aims inspiring much of the American resistance. It is a simple fact, however, that the growth and development of a nation depend upon the increase of its material production. The United States outstripped Great Britain in production long before World War I. But the growth of American influence abroad in terms of military power and imperial "rights," lagged far behind America's actual strength. Britain clung desperately to her first rank, to the shadow of power when the substance was gone. Clashes and near wars with Britain over this issue of who was really the strongest, took the form of conflicts over freedom of the seas. Impressment, one expression of British domination of the seas, had been a major cause of the War of 1812, but the war had not settled that issue, much less the issue of maritime freedom. In every war, British interference with American trade brought the United States to the boiling point. Even during the first two years of World War I, it was touch and go whether we would join Britain against Germany or declare war on Britain for her insolence on the high seas.

American naval power rose, during the first World War, to more than equality with Britain. Yet as late as 1929, the British still refused to acknowledge the change in the actual relation of forces, denying naval parity to the United States as a basis for Anglo-American agreement. It was only in 1930 that she yielded to threats of an armaments race in which America could easily prove its basic superiority. This marked the real end of the struggle: American power had overtaken British power. We would not have to ask freedom of the seas; we could enforce freedom for our ships—and deny it to others. Since British rule was founded on seapower, naval parity ended the outward show of British supremacy. It also constituted a British admission of dependence upon the United States for the continued integrity of the British Empire.

Only if that is understood is it possible to comprehend what went on behind the back of World War II. The United States drive to supplant Great Britain as the dominant power in the world—key to the whole of American history—has been hidden from the popular view in all its decisive stages. The rise of a more aggressive challenger, Germany, and the joint battles of America and Britain to put down the upstart, concealed from the public what was happening between the two allies. As a result of World War I, the United States acquired the dominant economic position in the world, Britain slipping into a poor second place. As a result of World War II, the United States acquired the corresponding strategic supremacy.

It is difficult to realize how abject a surrender to the United States was made by Winston Churchill while he was proudly holding a thumb aloft to boast that Britain would stand alone against Germany. It is easier if one starts with a realization of how hollow was the British shell of power. Britain had been living on borrowed time for fifty years, so far as her world status was concerned. The Anglophile, MacCormac, explains how she did it. As "the pioneer of the Industrial Revolution," she had a fifty-year headstart on all other nations. In this way, she "acquired a tremendous capital surplus" and invested it all over the world. She also built the world's major fleet and got the carrying trade. British merchants "established themselves at strategic points near the world's markets . . . London bankers discounted bills of exchange for all the world's traders and Lloyd's insured all the world's risks." This "beautifully integrated system" kept Great Britain in world economic and financial leadership for a half century after Germany and the United States had surpassed her in production, the true foundation of power. Britain was all bluff in 1940.

Churchill later boasted that he made it his whole policy to bring the United States into the war. He said nothing about the price he paid. A flock of books purporting to give the inside gossip on the strategy of World War II, have helped confuse the issue. Ralph Ingersoll's *Top Secret* is a good example. Ingersoll is bitter at what he sees as American knuckling under to Britain in matters of strategy. Such authoritative sources as Commander Butcher's *Eisenhower,* certainly confirm the charge that the United States frequently bowed to Churchill. They show that Anglo-American strategy, following Churchill's desire, tended to desert the Western Front where the war would inevitably be decided, in favor of strange maneuvers along the British Empire "life-lines." Anglo-American forces were scattered all over the world where, for the most part, they could have little weight in speeding the victory over Germany and Japan, much weight in deciding postwar distribution of power and territory as between Russia and Britain. This is where most of the so-called "hardboiled" discussion of Anglo-American relations during the war tends to stop.

It is true as far as it goes, but it goes something less than half the way. It ignores what the United States sought from Britain. Early in the war, the United States boasted that we had no mere second front, as the Russians urged, but a third, a fourth and a tenth front. This scattering of American forces added up to the War Department's postwar list of sixty countries, regions and major islands where American troops were stationed. As the Anglophobes say, this deployment of forces had more relation to postwar influence of Great Britain in the Mediterranean and South Asia than it had to winning the war. But the sixty American fronts — most of them remote from the decisive combat centers—had another meaning the Anglophobes neglect to mention: they spelled decisive strategic positions for the United States in a post war settlement with Great Britain. The settlement is still taking place, but it is not too early to say that its terms reduce Britain to permanent world inferiority.

That was the price Churchill paid. The Labor opposition dared not raise it against him even later in the course of the elections, for unless she were prepared to abandon her imperialist status, Britain had no alternative. She could surrender quietly to the United States, or shamefully to Germany. The first would mean American envelopment and penetration of the empire; the second would spell open surrender of her empire to the Germans. It would, moreover, mean world rule by a European power, certain to suppress any new challenge by Britain at an early stage, whereas the distant America might be less vigilant.

The virtual ousting of Britain from the American hemisphere, beginning with her surrender of Canada and completed by the military rapprochement of the United States and Argentina, was one of the more obvious costs of American aid. But it was a mere down payment. The ultimate price was surrender of British positions in the Atlantic and the Pacific which must spell like surrender of British claims on the continents across the two oceans. Loss of control over the oceans symbolized permanent surrender of the British Empire, permanent dependence upon the

United States for Britain's continued pretense of claim to world rank.

For the United States, winning of strategic supremacy in the hemisphere and the oceans on either side of it, promptly opened the way to much broader conquests. By assuming responsibility for rule of the Atlantic and Pacific, America automatically extended her commitments to every other body of land and water. The earlier-cited British Labor Party pamphlet emphatically affirmed that this was already the case. It stated without qualification that the United States has "undisputed control of *all* the oceans." And the whole British policy of retrenchment—with the consequent withdrawal from Greece that provided the occasion for launching the Truman Doctrine—is based on the relative decline of British seapower. As Anne O'Hare McCormick puts it, General Mark Clark's adventures in North Africa "brought the United States into the Mediterranean and opened the way to the great power shifts that tend to keep us there." But, she continues, the British voluntarily made the adjustments that these "power shifts" prepared.

"When they pulled up stakes in Greece, submitted the Palestine issue to the United Nations, started negotiations for the evacuation of Egypt—a more reluctant move because it trenches on the Sudan and the future of Africa—it was clear that they were deliberately easing out of their old place as a Mediterranean power."

It might be similarly shown that the British have not only accepted the impossibility of dominating the Indian Ocean or any other major body of water, but have been suspiciously eager to hasten transfer of control to the United States. The United States has not hesitated to take up these "obligations" even at those points most distant from our own shores. There are those who think this is a sucker's game, that in our time the old kind of imperialist rule can only produce more and bigger colonial revolts of the kind raging throughout Asia today. They think Britain has learned this costly lesson and is deliberately encouraging American imperialism to waste itself in the hopeless struggle to take over Britain's now untameable ex-subjects.

Such thoughts may be encountered here, in Britain, or anywhere else in the world. The important Chinese newspaper, *Ta Kung Pao* recently wrote: "Two years ago Greece was still a baby on the lap of Britain. Today Greece is already a burden for America. How wise are the British!"

Thus the uncontrolled spread of American power may prove costly, in the end, not only to the American people but to that very handful of economic interests, Big Navy blusterers and patrioteers who are today drunk with dreams of world rule. In the meantime, however, they have succeeded in pushing American naval guns into every stream from the Arabian Sea to the Caribbean and from the Arctic Ocean to the Antarctic. It is all at our expense; if, by our silence, we incur responsibility for the consequences of this aggressive, militaristic and imperialist adventure, we ought at least to be aware it is going on. Then we will not be tempted to blame others for the world tensions and crises and wars that result from our own boundless expansion.

PART II: BOUNDLESS EXPANSION

CHAPTER 8

PROFIT AND POWER

You cannot set loose a tide of expansionism and expect it to stop three miles from the shores of Europe and Asia. Indeed, supremacy over the Atlantic and Pacific Oceans cannot be said to have been established until our network of island bases finds firm anchorage on the continents across the seas. That the wave of American expansion *has* swept us deep into both Europe and Asia is evident. But to rescue the meaning of that advance from the meaningless "morality" preached by the press, is a tremendous task. One could show that even while we are busy persuading ourselves of our matchless morality, we are preparing a record harvest of hate all over the world. The apologists for the new imperialism, however, take care of this contradiction by yelling "Liar" at anyone who refuses to shut his eyes to the truth. Their hypocrisy—Webster defines the word as meaning "the false pretense of moral excellence"—knows no limits. The only way to counter their barrage of platitudes is to dig out the facts of American infiltration, domination and exploitation in every part of the world.

A thorough job of that kind could easily reach encyclopedic proportions. Nor is the story spread openly on the record in such areas, new to American domination, as Europe. I have therefore undertaken in this and the three following chapters, to describe modern American imperialism, not in abstract theoretic terms, but as it developed in the Far East. There the record of American participation in the scramble for imperialistic power and profit is long and documented. I have, then, taken the Far East simply as a model of the modern process of penetration, domination and exploitation.

Our extensive claims in the Far East today are the logical continuation of our long fight for Pacific supremacy. After all, American mastery of the Pacific was never an end in itself; it was a means. The profits to be gained from all the islands of that ocean, could not repay the immense cost of establishing and maintaining United States hegemony over 70,000,000 to 100,000,000 square miles of water surface against all Great Power rivals. Not even the limited banker-industrialist clique that spurs the search for overseas opportunities would have found the game worth the candle. But beyond the Pacific Ocean lies Asia, the principal prize of imperialism for the past three hundred years. Domination of Asia was the end to be attained by means of American conquest of the Pacific. The endless uses for idle capital in lands where labor is cheaper than life, the control of raw materials for home industry, the profits of trade, these were a Svengali-lure for the Wall Street Trilbies, as for their opposite numbers in London.

TRADE BY COMPULSION

The contest among the powers for the grand prize, is loosely summed up in the history of rivalry for "the China trade." The great scramble for control of China began in the 1830's when merchant capitalism yielded to industrial capitalism in Great Britain. Before that, China had indeed been trading with the British for 150 years, but in a manner and on a scale inconsistent with the greatly expanded production and market-hunger of England after the industrial revolution. The trade was a monopoly on both sides: for England, the British East India Company; for China, the Co-Hung, a merchant group under government supervision. The free trade Reform Act of 1832, however, was quickly followed in England by parliamentary abolition of the East India Company's monopoly, and the hitherto thwarted British merchants rushed into the Far East to grab what they could. Americans saw what was happening and joined in the stampede, for they, too, had been trading with Canton from the time of the Revolution.

With so many foreign merchants looking for business, the Co-Hung was a nuisance and, in general, Chinese imperial restrictions on trade chafed the Westerners. As Professor Taylor sees it, the industrial revolution, the principles of free trade and the practice of free competition, "made the great naval powers, particularly Great Britain and the United States, intolerant of the commercial policies of China and Japan. John Quincy Adams put his finger on the real issue: China and Japan had to be brought into the world market for our good, not their own."

The British, with more production and more shipping than we had, put this noble principle of compulsion into effect before we did. The first Anglo-Chinese war took place in 1842. We wasted little time, however, in following up the British blow; in 1844 we compelled the Chinese to grant us all the privileges the British had won by fighting. In 1853, we beat the British to the punch by opening Japan ourselves. Thus we went along with the British and fought them at the same time. Accordingly, we put into practice the "theory that if the Chinese, and later the Japanese, did not wish to trade with us according to our ideas they would be compelled to do so. That they were compelled is a matter of history." Our difference with the British was simply on the matter of whether we or they were to gather the harvest. For all our vogue for fine phrases about "Christianizing" and "Americanizing" the Chinese and Japanese, the real issue was profit and the power to extract profit.

Thus the use of violence against Asiatics to compel them to our will, was the very foundation of "business opportunity" in the Far East, for the Americans as for Europeans. There is no other word than "imperialism" to describe this process, yet our Pharisees find face to describe it as a "civilizing mission." Paullin smugly remarks that Japan, China, Korea, Turkey and other victims of American naval diplomacy, "may be classed together" as "backward, undeveloped and non-Christian countries . . . outside the pale of occidental civilization," and not even belonging "to the great family of nations." For such primitives, naval diplomacy was suitable; the naval officer "could best unite force with persuasion."

Our national understanding has been corrupted by this combination of hypocrisy and brutality. As Foster Rhea Dulles says, "It has always been difficult for the United States to know just where it stands, with principle ever warring against expediency, protestations of altruism denied by an aggressive nationalism. Just as in Hawaii and Samoa we again and again foreswore territorial ambitions and moved steadily toward ultimate control of those parts of the islands which we really coveted, so have we always decried imperialism while creating an empire." Though these are the words of a generally anti-annexationist writer, very similar language is employed by frankly expansionist Professor Taylor who is all-out for "Americanizing" the Far East. "The United States always sought to limit the imperialistic expansion of European powers while at the same time, as in China, insisting upon an equal share in the imperialistic position. This contradiction in American policy was naturally much more apparent to other countries than to the United States itself."

After the middle of the century, world developments hastened the clash of interests in China. Not only did Germany and Italy achieve national unification around 1870, but the growth of industry in those countries as well as in France and the United States, quietly ended Britain's long monopoly of world trade and world affairs. A furious race for colonies and territory began; strategic positions, positions often taken to keep them out of a rival's hands rather than for their exploitation value, were seized at will. Between 1878 and 1898 the whole of Africa was carved up. With the world completely partitioned and divided, the rivalry in China reached war heat.

There, as elsewhere, the British monopoly was plainly doomed. True, the British were long to remain in control of the Chinese customs. And Britain had a sphere of influence in the Yangtze Valley that embraced a third of China proper. Of China's foreign trade, 65 per cent was with Britain and 85 per cent was carried by British ships. But in the 1880's, the Russian trans-Siberian railroad brought Russia to the borders of Manchuria and outflanked Britain's naval control of China, so to speak. France penetrated Indo-China and began working her way north; Germany also put in her bid for Pacific power and possessions; and Japan, emerging with startling rapidity as a Great Power, decided that Korea, Manchuria, Mongolia, Formosa and the whole of China were her logical spheres.

By making war on China in 1894, Japan not only made her first bid for empire, but altered power relations throughout the world far more than she understood. China was, of course, helpless. At the peace negotiations, Japan demanded that China give up all claims to Korea, cede Formosa, the Pescadores and the Liaotung Peninsula (where Port Arthur and Dairen are located), the key to Manchuria. Germany and France, however, backed up Russia in forcing Japan to get out of Liaotung and accept a huge cash indemnity from China instead. This left Russia free to overrun Korea and Manchuria, which she did. Each move of this kind stirred each of the other powers into grabbing something else and the slicing continued right into 1898.

The clashes and greedy claims of all these powers jarred the United States out of its quietly acquisitive way, suddenly confronting capitalist America with the apparent choice of openly joining in the grab or being forever left out of the distribution of foreign markets. "The tendency of the businessmen and diplomats was, quite naturally, to seek exclusive commercial and financial privileges within their respective spheres," A. Whitney Griswold notes in *The Far Eastern Policy of the United States.* We might have known this from our own careful skimming of the economic cream in Hawaii. But if we were deceived, as to Hawaii, by our own moralizing, we were to get a quick lesson in Asia.

The lesson ran like this: As the Russians moved into Manchuria, private American interests decided there was room for them, too, in the exploitation of that rich territory. Standard Oil and the British-American Tobacco Company already had a foothold but in 1895 the very flower of American capitalism made a bid, with the full assistance of Washington, for economic conquest of the area. A syndicate including the Chase National Bank, the Bank of America, the American Sugar Refining Company, the ten largest American railroads and other interests, sought a concession to build Manchurian railways to connect with the Trans-Siberian. Railways are not merely one of the principal forms of investment in colonial countries, but as military-strategic keys to domination they tend to give the builder a growing claim to a sphere of influence and, ultimately, a monopoly of opportunity in the areas served by the railroad. Asking the Russians to let American interests have the profit and the power that go with railroad building, was equivalent to asking them to surrender Manchuria to the United States. That meaning is emphasized by State Department records recently opened to scholars, which say the proposed concession went beyond railroads, claiming for the United States "the right to exploit mines and forests in Manchuria and in the adjacent sections of Mongolia." In effect, the government, or the private interests employing the good offices of the State Department, thought we could buy an exclusive sphere of influence embracing Manchuria, Mongolia and North China, while Russia "had her hands full at home" as one American diplomat put it. Failing to obtain the concession, the Americans proposed to the Russians that they borrow the necessary funds for development of Manchuria from the syndicate—with such strings as might be attached. The United States was surprised and annoyed when the Russians said coldly that they had "no intention of turning to any foreign syndicate whatsoever." In 1896 the Russians themselves obtained a concession to build the Chinese Eastern Railway across Manchuria.

It was no better in the British sphere of influence or anywhere else in China where the British could block efforts of American interests to get railroad concessions. As the American diplomat, Charles Denby,* wrote to Secretary of State Sherman on April 2, 1897, "Our worst antagonists in the building of railroads or furnishing supplies are the English. I venture to state that there is not an English railroad man in China who does not attack, denounce and belittle American locomotives and the American railroad system."

From such experiences as these, American interests could see that in the event of the break-up of China, that vast empire would be parcelled out among the powers to the exclusion of the United States, and each power would retain the monopoly of trade and investment in its own area. The British said openly that a sphere of influence was a region "earmarked" to show that "in case of a breakup England did not wish any other power to have it." The well-founded fear of exclusion from the Asiatic market

---

* *Note to third edition:* In previous editions, Edwin Denby, son of Charles, was incorrectly named here. I am indebted to F. R. Wilson of Alger, Michigan, for the correction.

began to play a growing role in the thinking of American policy-makers.

This fear was exploited by a handful of highly-placed Americans — Theodore Roosevelt, Assistant Secretary of the Navy, Henry Cabot Lodge, chairman of the Senate Foreign Relations Committee, and Admiral Mahan who molded the thinking of Lodge, Roosevelt and a generation of imperialists. They urged the United States into the war with Spain and into subsequent annexation of the bulk of Spain's remaining possessions.

Our war with Spain further unsettled all power relations, precipitating new territorial scrambles in Asia, and this in turn still further stimulated our own appetite — a chain reaction. On March 6, 1898, Germany — with whom we had been near blows at Samoa some years earlier and on bad terms generally—seized Kiaochow in China. Russia took possession of Port Arthur and Talienwan on March 27; Great Britain matched this by seizing Weihaiwei April 2; France, not to be outdone, took Kwang Chow Bay April 22. Was it a mere coincidence that Admiral Dewey won his smashing victory at Manila on May 1?

It is true that all the grabbing did not immediately move the American general public or reverse our official policy. Two days after Germany's seizure of Kiaochow, President McKinley turned down a British suggestion that the United States join England "in the defense of China's territorial integrity," because "he was yet unable to see in the concessions-scramble any jeopardy to American trade." But if McKinley and the general public were slow to excite, that thin stratum of American life which has been decisive in the shaping of our national policies, was very much concerned about the carving up of China. On the eve of the Russian acquisition of Port Arthur, the American charge d'affaires in Peking (Peiping) wrote despairingly to Washington: "The greatest markets of the world, which we are just grasping, will be lost to us."

In the increasingly expansionist mood of 1898, American bankers, industrialists and statesmen were not at all ready to write off "the greatest markets in the world" as a loss. On the contrary, they cast the die for decisive entry into the Asiatic- and world-scramble for possessions, power and profits. With Dewey's victory as a foundation, a frank program of imperialist expansion was put before the American people. For the first time in American history there was brought forward for public debate the proposition that the United States was not beyond the reach of the great law of capitalism — expand or die. It was urged that we annex the Philippines and prepare to go further because the growth of American production must soon bring the day when a larger market and greater maneuvering space would no longer be a mere convenience but a vital need. The discussion lasted from perhaps 1898 to 1905; the basic thesis of the discussion became a permanent, if sometimes concealed, foundation of our foreign policy.

Wolf von Schierbrand said, in his *America, Asia, and the Pacific*: "The American expansion in the Pacific, immensely favored as it will be by the opening of the Panama Canal, is not a mere whim, not a thing merely desirable, but something absolutely necessary to safeguard our further national development, to preserve us from the curse of ill-balanced production generally called over-production and all its attendant evils . . . The United States has all the advantages, qualifications and some of the ambitions necessary for the mastery of the Pacific."

The ambitions were right on the surface. In the wave of American expansionism, the advocates of imperialism were forced to say plainly what they wanted. They wanted to annex an empire. Annexation or withdrawal from the Philippines was the issue of the 1900 elections. The Republicans stood for annexation, and it was made clear that Asiatic empire, not mere possession of the Philippines themselves, was the true objective of the program. Frank A.

Vanderlip, then Assistant Secretary of the Treasury, enthused:

"It is as a base for commercial operations that the islands seem to possess the greatest importance. They occupy a favored location, not with reference to any one part of any particular country of the Orient, but to all parts. Together with the islands of the Japanese Empire, since the acquirement of Formosa (by Japan), the Philippines are the pickets of the Pacific, standing guard at the entrance to trade with the millions of China, Korea, French Indo-China, the Malay Peninsula, and the Islands of Indonesia to the South."

John Barrett, former Minister to Siam and a correspondent in the Philippines during the war with Spain, added: "We would have an unsurpassed point in the Far East from which to extend our commerce and trade and gain our share in the immense distribution of material prizes that must follow the opening of China, operating from Manila as a base as does England from Hongkong."

Senator Beveridge declaimed: "And just beyond the Philippines are China's illimitable markets." Nor did he stop there. "The Power that rules the Pacific is the Power that rules the world. And with the Philippines that Power is and will forever be the American Republic."

Senator Mark Hanna, boss of the Republican Party and the man behind President McKinley, summed it up with the remark: "If it is commercialism to want the possession of a strategic point giving the American people an opportunity to maintain a foothold in the markets of that great Eastern country, for God's sake let us have commercialism."

Trade, commerce, sound innocent enough. But this is no world for innocents or innocence. The spokesmen for trade with China automatically employ military terms in their plea. A capitalist foothold in the East meant rivalry with other capitalists; an American foothold meant a long fight with Britain, France, Germany, Russia and Japan.

It was as a strategic base for ultimate armed conflicts to decide dominance of China, that the Philippines were sought. Admiral Mahan spoke frankly of our "Asiatic dominion" and described this series of acquisitions as "the widest sweep, in space, of our national extension." The United States, Professor Taylor observes, had become an imperial power, not so much for the sake of having an empire "as to neutralize the spread of other empires." This tendency to expand in order to prevent the expansion of others, (or to use that excuse), is a characteristic feature of modern one-world imperialism. In the debate over the Philippines, fear of German acquisition of bases in some part of the archipelago, helped carry the day for total annexation (as against the proposal that we take only Luzon). Whatever the shadings of motive, American commitments were so far and so rapidly extended over the globe that, in the words of Walter Lippmann, they "could be validated in the last analysis only by successful war." Which is to say that if we continued on the same path, we should ultimately have to fight for supremacy in Asia.

CHAPTER 9

THE OPEN DOOR

The United States was certainly not ready for war with the great powers to decide the mastery of Asia. But it was surely committed to seek that mastery. As a result of the public debate over annexation of the Philippines, the American public—for once—was more or less informed on the broad meaning of the act. United States acquisition of the Philippines was everywhere understood as shaking an American fist at the powers in the Far East. If we were not prepared for an immediate challenge, then diplomacy must be our weapon, but force is the iron fist beneath the glove of diplomacy, and all the variations of American policy in China from 1898 to 1948 pursued the single ultimate goal of supremacy in Asia.

Our diplomats, and private interests conducting their own diplomacy, were not always conscious of or concerned with the ultimate goal. But they did aim at something more than the profits of single transactions. All our diplomacy, by the very nature of the struggle in China, was directed toward obtaining permanent positions; political rights were inseparable from economic gains in the trade treaties and concessions, and political-economic gains sooner or later fused into strategic positions.

So it was with our much misunderstood and deliberately glamorized policy of the Open Door in China which we initiated immediately following the annexation. The policy has been text-booked as one of high moral opposition to the carving-up of China; it has been painted as a doctrine of opposition to closed spheres in the interest of abstract justice, out of regard for the Chinese, and with the desire for fair play to all trading nations. But we have already seen that foreign policies in China were never concerned with the "good" of China or the Chinese.

It is easy enough to dispose of the pretense in this case. The study several times previously cited, in which American financial policy abroad was examined under the direction of banker Lamont, drily points out that at the moment we were demanding the Open Door from the dominant powers in the Far East, we were closing the door in our own sphere of interest in the Caribbean and banging it shut in everybody's face in the Philippines. And these diverse and mutually contradictory principles nevertheless "worked to the advantage of American private financial interests in the regions where they have been actually applied." Hence, the study concludes:

"The stated purpose of the department was to establish the 'Open Door' in China, in financial as well as in commercial matters, and presumably for China's own benefit as well as for that of the American bankers and investing public. Actually, the episode was a part of Secretary Knox's 'dollar diplomacy,' the policy of extending the American financial empire in the more backward regions of the world by aggressive but non-military procedures."

What was true of the Open Door in the era of Dollar Diplomacy, was already true in 1899-1900 when the policy was first formulated. Its very origins demonstrate that it was the child of imperialism. As usual, it was Great Britain, not the United States, that invented the new formula. And, characteristically, the British did not become infatuated with the high principle until other States had broken their monopoly of power in China. In British practice, the Open Door was an attempt to restore the broken balance of power in the Far East and on a world scale. It was, in other words, an instrument of "power politics."

Germany was building naval power and diplomatic positions in Europe and Africa to challenge Britain to a showdown for world power. Anglo-French rivalry in the Nile Valley produced the Fashoda incident in 1898, which gave the whole world a war scare. In Asia, it was Russian power that threatened to crowd the British out of China and perhaps weaken their hold over India. The British had even had a very sharp public quarrel with the United States in 1895-1896 over the Venezuela boundary. "For a moment," says Griswold, "England stood alone, friendless, amid the ruins of her once 'splendid' isolation. Then, in a characteristically pragmatic fashion, her diplomats began a systematic effort to reestablish the balance of power wherever British interests demanded it."

The Open Door was but one of three simultaneous lines of diplomatic fence-mending employed by the British, and it was perhaps the least of the three. Outright participation in the scramble for economic and territorial concessions — the exact opposite of the Open Door — was one of the methods, though it was employed reluctantly and as a matter of prestige after 1896. The third and principal policy was that of bilateral negotiation with rivals, leading to the Anglo-Japanese alliance of 1902 and the *Entente Cordiale* (Anglo-Franco-Russian front against Germany) of 1904.

In common with the other two methods, the Open Door was directed toward easing the threats to the British spheres and British trade in China. Like the other methods, it sought to exploit antagonisms among her rivals to divide them while Britain strengthened herself with alliances. "To protect her lucrative Chinese markets from the closing pincers of France in the south and Russia in the north (allies since 1894), England took a new interest in the territorial integrity of China," Griswold writes with dry irony. "Territorial integrity" meant no more economic or territorial concessions to her rivals. That it also meant no more concessions to herself, was not an equal sacrifice: she had more than she could absorb or manage. The Open Door also meant abolition of discriminatory tariffs in all the spheres and concessions. This likewise favored Britain because her "unique position as money-lender and exporter to the world" would enable her to get more from her rivals' spheres than they would get from hers. In sum, the Open Door was a tactical move favoring Britain in the great game of "power politics" at just that time and place.

"Power politics" is a hissing phrase in our time. There is a stigma attached to the term. This is confusing, and the result of confusion. All foreign policies in a world of competition rest, ultimately, on force; that the power of a nation should be employed or felt in the achievement of its objectives is not wrong or immoral but inevitable. The special position of the United States, the Soviet Union, Great Britain, France and China in the United Nations today, for example, is but an acknowledgment of the fact of unequal power as a starting point for international relations.

It is *how* power is employed that determines the good or evil of a policy. And it is "power politics" employed for imperialist ends that we are dealing with here. It would be more accurate therefore, to say that *the Open Door policy as employed by Great Britain and inherited by the United States, was part of the diplomacy of imperialism. It was imperialist because its objectives were imperialist prizes. It was a policy designed to preserve and even extend foreign domination and exploitation of China and the Chinese.*

Griswold supplies an instance. In a secret note on February 3, 1898, "well over a year before the idea of collective action to guarantee the Open Door appears to have entered the head of an American diplomat," British Foreign Secretary Joseph Chamberlain outlined the Open Door policy to Prime Minister Arthur Balfour. He said: "Our Chinese policy is to be a declaration that any port occupied by a foreign nation shall be, *ipso facto*, a Treaty Port open to all on precisely similar conditions." In other words, all the foreign powers with strength enough to wrest a "Treaty Port" from China, should share all such imperialist prizes. But, "further, they should join with us in putting pressure on the Chinese — loan or no loan — to open Nanking and other Ports suggested by us and to give freedom of internal navigation." That is, the imperialist powers should act collectively to force China to surrender segments of her economy or fragments of her political independence not yet torn from her by the wolves.

Professor Taylor affirms that this imperialist character of the Open Door remained at the heart of the policy as continued by the United States. "The so-called Open Door, for example, *which was not open to China,* was an international agreement for equality of commercial opportunity in China. By international agreement China was compelled to accept a very low tariff over which foreign goods could be cheaply imported and China's raw materials cheaply exported." It was, in effect, a continuation of the old "theory" that China must be forced to trade not for her own good but for ours. The Open Door forced her to buy foreign goods and prevented her from taxing imports and exports to get revenues for industrialization and internal improvements. It operated like all other imperialist policies, to keep her indebted, her finances handled by foreigners to "protect" their debts, her ports occupied and administered by foreigners, her soil policed by foreign troops, her people debased, hungry and of short life.

This British imperialist Open Door policy was taken over by the United States in a curiously direct line. The Open Door notes dispatched by Secretary of State John Hay on September 6, 1899, were written by William W. Rockhill. But they were little more than a copy of memoranda supplied by Alfred E. Hippisley, a British citizen, who had been a member of the British-administered Chinese Imperial Customs Service since 1867. Rockhill acknowledged himself no more than the "mouthpiece" of Hippisley. The record of the long friendship and correspondence of Rockhill and Hippisley — who also presented his ideas directly to Secretary Hay — shows that the Hay circular of July 3, 1900 (completing the formulation of the American version of the Open Door), was Hippisley's work also.

A smug phrase, "Asking only the open door for ourselves, we are ready to accord the open door to others," is perhaps the first mention of the Open Door in an American diplomatic document. It appears in an instruction by President McKinley to American Peace Commissioners on September 16, 1898. How little this pious attitude has to do with the reality of imperialist rivalry in China! The Open Door notes and circular actually sought trade equality for the United States in the spheres already established by rival powers; they also attempted to stave off the disadvantageous (to us) partition of China among the powers.

Like the British parent policy, our Open Door was further designed to fasten the chains tighter on the common victim of the powers — China. Rockhill, for instance, immensely pleased with the adoption of his — or rather, Hippisley's — policy, expressed the hope that we would use our "balance of power" in China "for strengthening the Peking government so that it can find no means of escaping the performance of all its obligations to the treaty powers . . . China can and must discharge its international obligations." This is Open Doorese for a proposal to create a Chinese puppet government strong enough to put down all Chinese opposition to foreign financial extortion and concession-granting.

But it didn't work. The June, 1900, Boxer Rebellion against "foreign missionaries and concession-hunters," was also a blow at "the Manchu government that truckled with them." As Professor Taylor says, "it was China, not the United States, which prevented the process of partition from being completed. The Boxer Rebellion compelled the western powers to unite in the suppression of an anti-imperialist movement at the very moment when they were about to slice up the victim. Any continuation of the process of partition might well have ended in war . . . [So] they were persuaded to sign an international agreement with China, the Boxer Protocol, which established international control over China instead of the monopoly domination of any one power." Its effect was to "preserve the Chinese market for joint exploitation." Joint imperialist oppression instead of division of slices — that is all the great morality of the Open Door amounted to. And even that postponement of partition was not voluntary; the threat of further rebellion of the victim and the lack of strength by any one power to challenge all the others, dictated the pause.

The United States, of course, did not think of any immediate armed challenge to rival powers established in Asia before our time. Our seizure of the Philippines had given us a base for possible future challenge, but for the present it was, if anything, a strategic liability, an isolated outpost. Moreover, the break-up of the Spanish Empire under our blows, also benefited our rivals. Germany got the Caroline, Marshall and Palau Islands (destined to pass to Japan as "mandates" after War I and to the United States as a "trusteeship" after War II). Russia extended her influence in South Manchuria, in the adjustments of the period, by obtaining a railroad concession for a branch of the Chinese Eastern Railway from Harbin to Port Arthur. Our prospects in Asia were not good. Certainly we lacked strength for armed ouster of our rivals from the coveted spheres.

It was therefore inevitable that we should have turned to power politics and equally natural — given our long tradition — that we should have dressed our policy in the sheep's clothing of morality. But our Open Door foray into world politics gained us nothing. The policy won superficial international agreement, but it did not change power relations and, indeed, the agreement was no tribute to our power. As Griswold sums up the episode: "The Boer War, the German Navy, the maneuverings of the hostile European coalitions, the Czar, the Kaiser, Delcasse and

Salisbury—these were the factors and agents that called the halt, not the diplomacy of John Hay. It was a case of political stalemate rather than conversion to principle. No power dared move further for fear of precipitating the universal debacle that was to come a decade later . . ."

The United States recognized the failure of the Open Door to achieve the political and economic objectives it sought. Hippisley himself predicted that the Boxer settlement would end in "territorial concessions leading to partition and so to war among the powers." Rockhill wrote from China that he hoped "it may be a long time before the United States gets into another muddle of this description." And Hay, driven by the War and Navy Departments, did an about face from the Open Door to the policy of trying to grab territory. He sought an American naval base and territorial concession at Samsah Bay in the province of Fukien. But this happened to be in the Japanese sphere of influence and the Japanese said "No." They also crushed Colonel Hay by recalling his own moral strictures against using the Boxer Rebellion as an excuse for territorial aggrandizement.

"BALANCE OF POWER"

Thus ended our first Open Door adventure. The Open Door, as a phrase at least, remained a permanent part of our diplomatic arsenal especially in the Far East, but its content was never twice the same. The real meaning of our diplomacy changed from period to period and even varied from day to day during any given period. From the Hay notes to the Hay circular, for instance, we drastically revised our own concept of our own interpretation of the Open Door. Griswold points out that the notes not only took spheres of influence and territorial concessions for granted, but recognized that they would even expand "as is proved by the fact that the notes asked for most-favored-nation treatment for American commerce in all future as well as present spheres and leased territories." But the circular asked a guarantee against further slicing, and we were to vacillate between these two concepts of the Open Door for many, many years.

Under McKinley and Hay, nevertheless, the Open Door always represented essentially one thing: the feeble plea of a latecomer for a share in the already divided spoils of empire. It was the moral argument put forward when we had nothing stronger to use. But now came Theodore Roosevelt who had watched the Open Door game long enough and was unwilling to play it. He plunged the United States full into the poison-pool of imperialist intrigue, employing traditional European divide-and-win methods. The Open Door became a mere auxiliary instrument, its meaning dependent upon the state of affairs in the game he was playing.

Dominating his State Department, Roosevelt adapted to the Far East and to his estimate of American interest, the balance of power principle by which Britain had prevented her victims and rivals from uniting to break her world rule. Aiming specifically at American penetration of North China and Manchuria, as the most practicable United States sphere of influence in Asia, he determined to play Japan and Russia against one another as far as the game might go.

Following this line of thought, he reinforced the efforts of American private interests to get positions in Manchuria, by diplomatic blackmail. Russia was given to understand that while American public opinion would not countenance a declaration of war against her, we could easily set the Japanese at her throat.

"I take it for granted," Secretary Hay wrote to the President in 1903, "that Russia knows as we do that we will not fight over Manchuria, for the simple reason that we cannot . . . but they know that it would require the very least encouragement on the part of the United States or England to induce Japan to seek a violent solution of the question."

When Russia proved stubborn, the United States used its facilities to strengthen Japan, believing we could halt the process at a safe point. Then, American assurances of our "benevolent neutrality" plus Anglo-American financial aid to Japan under the direct inspiration of President Roosevelt, launched the Russo-Japanese War of 1904-5. Japan, having built a modern navy with the indemnity squeezed from China in 1895, easily defeated Russia, who had proved unable to develop Great Power strength at sea even to the extent of her purely defensive needs. The Russian fleet was, moreover, shattered at Port Arthur by a Pearl Harbor-attack without previous declaration of war.

President Roosevelt was well satisfied with his work. He gloated over the Port Arthur affair. "I was thoroughly well pleased with the Japanese victory," he said, and he told himself Japan was "playing our game" whether she would or not.

Neither love for Japan nor hatred for czarism, inspired American policy. American predominance in Manchuria was the simple goal. As Professor Edward H. Zabriskie writes, in *American-Russian Rivalry in the Far East, 1895-1914*, on the strength of first-hand access to State Department files, Roosevelt's "purpose was to give Japan a free hand in Korea, to render her assistance, both morally and financially in her fight to loosen the clutch of Russia in Manchuria, with its menace to American commercial and industrial interests, to prolong the war for a sufficient length of time to exhaust both Russia and Japan, and to leave a weakened Russia and a strengthened Japan facing each other at the end of the war, thereby equalizing the Manchurian balance of power. A war from which both powers would emerge financially, economically, and physically drained. . . . would better serve the economic and commercial interests of the American Republic."

The war was maintained as long as Britain and the United States—for very dissimilar reasons—wanted it to go on. That they had pretty absolute control, is indicated by the war financing—more than half the war's estimated billion dollar cost to Japan was raised by loans in New York and London. Roosevelt exercised his influence to end the war on terms that would not let Japan grow too strong. Though the United States was still, perhaps, least of the Great Powers in the day to day pursuit of imperialist prizes, though Roosevelt was childishly innocent of knowledge or understanding of the incredibly complex interrelations of imperialist diplomacy, the peace was reached on American-influenced terms. Something like a stalemate of the other Great Powers gave the United States a balance of power position in the matter. At any rate, the treaty was negotiated in the United States, to emphasize the desire of the United States for a dominant position in the disputed areas.

The treaty gave Japan Port Arthur and Dairen and the South Manchurian railway. The settlement also gave Japan *de facto* rule of Korea. This conformed roughly to the Roosevelt plan. It was supposed to create the desired balance of power, the stalemate that would let American interests take over Manchuria. Wall Street, therefore, in the person of railroad king Edward H. Harriman, immediately came along with a grandiose plan for an American-owned round-the-world railroad system. He approached the Russians and Japanese confidently, for he believed only American decision had saved the Russian Maritime Provinces from the Japanese at the peace negotiations, and, on the other hand, it was through his agency that Japan had obtained certain war loans from the New York bankers, Kuhn-Loeb and Company. He proposed to buy the Trans-Siberian and South Manchurian railways.

But it was all vanity. The far-reaching Roosevelt plan had been too clever by half. American power was not yet sufficiently great on a world or Pacific scale to be decisive in the final reckoning. The war and its settlement did not produce the expected result. As a Russian diplomat put it, it gave Manchuria two masters instead of one. And both masters said "No" to Harriman!

Instead, alarmed by the aggressiveness of American policy, the Japanese and Russians moved to patch up their relations as soon as the war was over. In 1907, a year of worldwide reshuffling of Great Power alliances, they completed the patching by signing open agreements which obviously meant a common front against American infiltration into Manchuria. Behind the open agreements there were the usual secret treaties. These conceded Korea to Japan, recognized Japan's sphere in South Manchuria and Inner Mongolia and confirmed Russia's sphere in North Manchuria and Outer Mongolia.

Roosevelt was forced to acknowledge failure of his diplomacy and to set about mending fences. In 1905, Secretary of War Taft, destined to be the next President of the United States, negotiated a secret memorandum with Japan. By this memorandum the United States recognized Japanese sovereignty in Korea, and Japan promised to respect our rule in the Philippines. Three years later, by the Root-Takahira agreement, Roosevelt, in effect, gave Japan a free hand in Manchuria for the same promise to keep away from the Philippines. An outgrowth of these two deals was the subsequent participation of American capital in the exploitation of Korea and South Manchuria. Thus fortified, the Japanese in 1910 formally annexed Korea without American protest. And thus, having learned that to play power politics you must have power, the United States turned away from Roosevelt's amateur imperialism to a game more suited to the rapidly growing financial power of America—Dollar Diplomacy.

CHAPTER 10

DOLLAR DIPLOMACY

What is "Dollar Diplomacy"? President Taft, who introduced it as a substitute for the methods of European imperialism which Roosevelt had unsuccessfully borrowed, provided a definition: "This policy has been characterized as substituting dollars for bullets. . . . It is an effort frankly directed to the increase of American trade upon the axiomatic principle that the government of the United States shall extend all proper support to every legitimate and beneficial American enterprise abroad."

Though Taft spoke of "trade," in truth investment had replaced trade as the principle ingredient of capitalism's foreign adventures. Department of Commerce studies show that Taft took office at the beginning of the second great period of expansion of direct American investments abroad (the first having been from 1898 to 1902; this one lasted from 1908 to 1915, while a third was to follow from 1920 to 1929; and we are now apparently completing a fourth which began in 1939).

But Dollar Diplomacy is not simply the diplomacy of investment. It is, on the record, a method of conquering strategic positions by use of financial influence. In that sense, it is preeminently the diplomacy of the United States and there is no comparable Pound Diplomacy, or Franc Diplomacy or Mark or Yen Diplomacy, though all of these had their role in the narrower sense of investment diplomacy. The United States had no true rival because this type of financial diplomacy entered world affairs just when the United States was beginning the final climb to peaks of financial power never scaled by the British at the height of their own economic, political and military-strategic ascendancy.

Taft's definition implies a moral superiority of Dollar Diplomacy. It is unnecessary to argue whether it would really be morally better for the world if the old evils of imperialism, imposed by the power of bullets, were to be perpetuated solely by the power of dollars. It is unnecessary because history has already demonstrated that dollars are not a substitute for force but an adjunct of force. The flag follows the dollar. After Taft came a whole series of Marine interventions in the Western Hemisphere, and the pursuit of power was not left to bankers and missionaries in Asia, either.

Watching Dollar Diplomacy at work, one wonders that anyone would find words of praise for it. In China, for instance, during and after Taft's time, the characteristic feature of Dollar Diplomacy has been the openness of Wall Street's connection with the State Department. In fact, the two seem almost to merge at times, the same persons now officially representing the United States, now working directly for the American bankers with the aid of the State Department. Willard Straight, an outstanding name in the history of American empire-building efforts in the Far East, went from college in 1901 to the British-operated Imperial Chinese Maritime Customs Service, thence to the American diplomatic service, thence to the service of the banks, and back again to the State Department.

It really made no difference. While a diplomatic underling at Seoul, Korea, he had already "come to the conclusion," according to Griswold, "that the United States owed its lack of power in the Far East to the small amount of American capital invested in China." Trade didn't have the same tendency as investment to establish "the proprietary rights that constituted the entering wedge for political influence." So, as a diplomat, Straight saw nothing improper in working to increase Wall Street's influence; from 1906 to 1908 he "made his Mukden consulate a high-pressure sales agency for American commerce in Manchuria" and schemed with Harriman to build the latter's pet round-the-world railroad. Thereafter, "as Acting Chief of the Far Eastern Division, he worked for Harriman and as Harriman's representative, he worked for the State Department." Next, J. P. Morgan and Company was brought in to head an American financial group including the First National Bank, the National City Bank, Harriman, and Kuhn, Loeb and Company. When this group became the official agent of the Department of State for American railway financing in China, what more natural than that Willard Straight should be hired as the bankers' Peking representative?

Apologists of American imperialism are fond of arguing that the bankers didn't urge the State Department to forward their interests and get them investment opportunities in China; the shoe was on the other foot. Griswold cites instances from Taft to Wilson, and concludes that Dollar Diplomacy "was an attempt to force American capital by diplomatic pressure into a region of the world where it would not go of its own accord."

This may be accurate enough if you look so closely at the diplomatic trees that you cannot see the imperialist forest. But if you stand away, you will see that the growth of surplus capital at home was more and more determining both the domestic and foreign policy of the United States, pushing American policy in the direction of foreign expansion, increase of foreign investment, as the very heart of "the national interest." The theory of the virtues of "private enterprise" or "business," as taught in schools, churches, newspapers, makes the interests of "business" identical with the interests of the nation. The bankers and industrial barons are our national heroes. So it was that Straight came by his early conviction that our bankers must expand their investments in China, as the foundation for political domination by the United States. Federal, local and State governments as well as the State Department, the Army and Navy, all tend to operate according to this same prevailing concept of "the national interest." No wonder it was so easy for the same persons to move now to Wall Street, now to Washington. Or for the State Department to follow the lead of Wall Street today while tomorrow urging a reluctant Wall Street to take a more active role in a region where the American bankers had little experience or little interest.

That the men in the State Department and White House should from time to time be ahead of the bankers in desire for entry of American private interests to a given region, has still another meaning. The bankers are engaged with their immediate affairs; it is the business of the diplomats to take the long view. The banker's tendency is to invest only where he can see immediate profit or at least where politically stable conditions promise him constant control of the business he establishes abroad. It is the capitalist statesman's job to see that American positions are established that will add up to political influence eventually, even if that requires unprofitable investment today. It is the question of power.

Thus when Griswold argues that "Dollar Diplomacy had been contrived more as a political instrument than as the answer to the express needs of American business; it was the servant of a theory, not the supply to a demand," he does not succeed in clearing private capital of the charge of expansionism. He merely demonstrates that diplomacy is the handmaiden of surplus capital, preparing the way for its future placement abroad. Diplomacy sets the stage for strategic expansion to the ultimate benefit of private interests which might otherwise neglect these more distant opportunities out of preoccupation with present profits.

The very nature of the major imperialist investments in China shows that strategic expansion lies at the heart of the matter. The great battle of Dollar Diplomacy was for railroad concessions and a share in loan-making where political controls accompanied the loans. Railroads are not just profitable investments; they spell economic control over the life of a country. But that isn't all. Railroads are of decisive strategic significance. By their nature, transportation and communications — railroads, airlines, radio, telegraph, even news — are major military assets. As Oliver J. Lissitzyn notes in his *International Air Transport and National Policy*:

"A fact of cardinal importance in the relations between governments and the means of transportation and communication is that governments have not been able or willing to consider the operation of such means as just another private business. Nor have governments restricted their interest in these means to economic considerations alone. Throughout history political and military objectives have been inseparable from economic considerations."

If the means of transportation and communications are instruments of power, state-control, direct or indirect, becomes inevitable. Railroads, at home and abroad, airlines, telecommunications, even news agencies — worldwide businesses by their nature — are subsidized by all governments in our time, and their economic aspects are subordinated to their use as instruments of national policy.

The aviation aspect of this problem is familiar to everyone today. Pan-American Airways, for instance, is a nominally private system that is really a state agency. William A. M. Burden, then special aviation assistant to the Secretary of Commerce, wrote in 1943 (*The Struggle for Airways in Latin America*), that the "Pan-American System can be compared with the leading European government-owned or -controlled airlines in that it is the only operator representing the interests of its country in the international field and to this end is liberally subsidized by the United States." Two or more "competing" lines may also be molded into one state instrument. The wartime value of aviation determines peacetime "civil" aviation policies. Our control of the internal civil airlines of many countries, including China, spells strategic domination over those countries, and strategic domination brings the power to manipulate and exploit the land and its people.

That was the objective of the United States' battle for railway concessions in China. For instance, in 1916, taking advantage of the war in Europe, the United States made deals in the interest of American control of Chinese communications. The American International Corporation contracted to do drainage and irrigation work on the Huai River and part of the Grand Canal; the Siems and Carey Corporation got a concession for the most extensive railway network ever schemed up for China. That American control of these communications would have struck out at every rival position in China, was promptly indicated by the protests. All the European powers joined Japan in blocking the deals. Japan opposed the canal project as threatening her proposed seizure of Shantung, hitherto German-dominated. Russia protested the proposed railway extending into Mongolia; England forbade rail lines in Hupeh, Hunan and Szechuan; France banned another in Kwangsi.

There is an immediate connection between the American tendency to plot China-wide economic plans and the American diplomacy of "equality of opportunity," "territorial and administrative integrity" of China. The United States, alone of the powers, had the resources to attempt exploitation of the whole country. Britain could not even fully utilize her Yangtze sphere of influence, comprising a third of China proper. The pressure of the United States was therefore designed to strike out interest-lines and convert China into one great American sphere of influence. Secretary of State Lansing, for instance, protesting the interference of the powers, told the British that their attitude was "at variance with the policy of the 'Open Door' and equality of commercial opportunity to which the British government has subscribed."

The other powers could defend themselves only by still

further tightening their grip on their special cuts of the imperialist pie. Arthur Balfour accordingly replied that things had changed in China so that now "specific areas are earmarked for the enterprise of specific countries" and there could be no such thing as "a regime of free railway construction." He might have added that Britain couldn't permit such a competitive regime, because all railway concessions were bought with bribes and the United States could pay bigger bribes. Hippisley had once told Rockhill and Hay that railway and mining concessions "have usually been granted to those who were most liberal in greasing the palms of the middlemen."

Times had indeed changed. The phraseology of the Open Door, that once expressed late-arriving America's plea for a share of the China trade, had now become the demand of a financial giant for surrender, by lesser financial powers, of their private empires in China, so that he might have the whole. No power could voluntarily yield to this demand, and, frightened by it, all were able to compose their own differences just enough to present a common front against the United States. As a result, the United States suffered apparent failure in all its efforts to break down the established spheres of influence in China until the end of World War II.

The United States never tired of repeating its demand for the Open Door — and never ceased recognizing and dealing with the closed ones. Early in 1920, Thomas W. Lamont went to Japan as agent of the American banking group involved in the long history of Far East multi-power combinations known as "consortiums." On March 30, he forwarded to Secretary of State Colby a plan which thereupon became the plan of the United States Government. According to his and Colby's since-published notes, Lamont reached agreement with the Japanese bank group on formation of a British, French, American, Japanese consortium, in which Japan would waive "mention of any general economic or political rights in Manchuria and Mongolia." This looked like the Open Door. But the railways and mines dominated by the Japanese, were excluded, by name, from the scope of the agreement. In other words, the Japanese did not insist on specific mention of their closed sphere, so long as there was specific mention of every economic asset in the sphere. The door was not even ajar.

OUR WAITING GAME

It would be easy to conclude that we were getting nowhere, that our diplomacy and attempts at "power politics" were adventures without roots or fruits. Griswold comes to that conclusion. He remarks that "the history of American diplomacy in the Far East from 1903 to 1938 recapitulates in a series of cycles the experience of John Hay. One after another, with variations only in manner and emphasis, the Presidents and Secretaries of State who followed McKinley and Hay have moved toward identical objectives, with identical results"—tactical retreat and admitted failure. But Griswold again fails to take the long view.

It is perfectly true that our diplomacy was naive beyond belief. In the competition with powers long familiar with the intricate balance of forces behind the diplomacy of imperialism, skilled to detect the decisive European interests behind mysterious maneuvers in the Far East, Hay, Roosevelt and their successors suffered a succession of humiliating defeats. It is true, however, only of the short-term objectives of their diplomacy.

In the long run, it was question of power on a world scale that would determine the victory in Asia. Financial power was becoming more and more the inward measure of power in general, and that inward power had a tendency to find outward expression in bases, naval ratios, military-strategic dominance of new areas. The financial pre-eminence of the United States was growing behind the scenes and at periods of crisis it was rapidly transformed into military-strategic power. If we appeared to be thwarted in Asia, that was but the appearance. The reality of our financial power was a worldwide phenomenon; it might take time to find expression in Asia, but it would find it.

It did. The Washington Conference in 1922 marked the real arrival of American supremacy—in the conflict of rival imperialisms—not only in the Pacific but in Asia, though we were to wait twenty-five years for the outward proofs. The mere fact that the United States could call the conference, could assert leadership, was an indication of the change in comparative strengths of the powers, quickened by the war. The results of the conference represented an acknowledgement by Britain and Japan of our new supremacy.

"The British were compelled to give up the Anglo-Japanese alliance," observes Professor Taylor, "and the Japanese to get out of Shantung." In so doing they were immediately avoiding a naval race with the United States, which they could not but lose; but they were also acknowledging past demonstrations of the growth of American power. For the United States had more and more devoted its strength to publicly checking and driving back the Japanese in East Asia. Though Secretary Lansing and almost the whole State Department were blinded by anti-Bolshevik fury in 1918, the policy of the United States as it emerged from the conduct of General Graves, commander of American forces in Siberia, fully backed by President Wilson, was to prevent the Japanese from gaining strength by seizure of Russian territory in Asia. The 1922 agreement at Washington was a treaty-acknowledgement that the power of the United States had grown so great that even across the Pacific, in East Asia, it was sufficient to block the plans of Japan, despite the latter's tremendous geographic advantage.

The 1922 conference results were summarized in the fixing of the so-called 5-5-3 ratio for naval tonnage — equality of Britain and the United States, inferiority for Japan. Worldwide equality of Britain and the United States, meant tacit British surrender of the Pacific to the United States, since Britain must keep much strength near home. What it might mean in terms of relative American-Japanese strength in the Western Pacific, remained to be proved. But there is no reason to doubt that American banker-diplomats and sailor-diplomats and professional diplomats alike based their reasoning on the obviously continuing growth of American economic, financial, and military-strategic power.

That is why it is narrow and unrealistic to treat our Asiatic policy and diplomacy as a succession of failures in an attempt to assure the integrity of China for the good of the Chinese. There was no such attempt; there could be no such failure. What we sought was the domination of China as a whole for the advantages that would yield to American private interests (whether American capitalism, as such, would benefit or whether only a few favored interests, is irrelevant). Our long-range policy toward China and the whole Far East may be described with the brutal candor Secretary Bayard employed in speaking of Hawaii during President Cleveland's first administration. Our policy, he said, was "to wait quietly and patiently and let the islands fill up with American planters and American industries until they should be wholly identified with the United States. It was simply a matter of waiting until the apple should fall."

We could not literally fill China with American planters; and combinations of rivals limited the extent of penetration of American industries and finance. But we could and did accumulate overwhelming power on a world scale. The increasingly wide margin of American industrial supremacy, the staggering reserves of capital, the superiority of American technology, awaited only another war to be cashed in for strategic expansion in Asia on a limitless scale. That is to say, as between the United States and all imperialist rivals, relative strengths were so changing as to assure the final victory of America in the contest for the "right" to dominate and exploit the Far East. But always and behind that, the forces of resistance to all imperialism were growing at a still more rapid rate. Victory was in sight for our own imperialists—but for those who looked close it was a hollow victory ahead.

APPEASEMENT

The content of our Far Eastern ripe-fruit policy—our waiting game—was solidly imperialistic. We did not employ the Open Door and repeated demands for preservation of "the territorial and administrative integrity" of China, to crack the central structure of foreign domination over China. We employed them only to maintain a legal wedge for swift American penetration of the British, Japanese and other spheres when power-relations should change. We were preparing to break down the barriers and take as our inheritance all that the diplomacy of European imperialism had built up in the Far East.

This policy involved confirming, and even trying to "freeze" the imperialist *status quo* in the Pacific and Far East, whereas the Chinese people wanted at all cost to keep up their fierce fight and shake the foundations of foreign rule. China refused, for instance, to sign the Versailles treaty, or, as Griswold remarks: "It would be more accurate to say that the ruling faction at Peking was restrained from dealing directly with Japan because of the extreme [popular] opposition to this course." Spontaneous boycotts of Japanese goods became a powerful political and diplomatic weapon for China; the armed struggle for national liberation might well have been encouraged then rather than fifteen years later. Instead, we virtually forced China to sign the 1922 treaties confirming Japan's, Britain's, and our own positions.

President Harding told the Chinese Minister "it would be a colossal blunder in statecraft" to refuse the treaties, "as the alternative might involve a risk of losing" Shantung. But Shantung *was* lost to China, in effect, by the treaty of February 4, 1922, which she signed under American and British pressure. Griswold says it "restored Shantung in full sovereignty to China but by virtue of the terms of the Japanese railway loan, did not greatly disturb Japan's economic supremacy (and concomitant political influence) in the province." This was agreeable to the British, for they and the French "were no more willing to relinquish their Chinese spheres and leaseholds than was Japan."

As for us, we were following the British lead in the traditional manner, though with our own objectives. Just as the Englishman, Hippisley, gave us our Open Door policy, so Arthur Balfour's draft of November 11, 1921 became the Nine Power Treaty of February 6, 1922, presented to the world as an American initiative. The several treaties and agreements binding the powers not to fortify certain Pacific positions, did not mean that the United States "had decided to abandon American interests in China. It meant, rather, that Hughes had decided to employ a traditional as opposed to a radical method of defending those interests." It meant joining the powers in maintaining imperialist domination over China, while putting forward our claims against the existing spheres.

The very nature of imperialist rivalry confirms that our policy was a waiting game. "The treaties of Washington," Griswold explains, "were primarily a recognition of existing, if brutal, facts, a consolidation of the *status quo*. By them the Pacific suffered no peaceful change; it was only partially frozen. The same was true of China." By them the United States, not ready for war, "went as far as pen and ink could go" to contain Japan and "to preserve a peace founded on such antithetical elements as those inherent in the *status quo* in the Far East."

Lenin put the same thing more bluntly long ago. He said imperialists cannot make peace; they can only establish a truce from time to time acknowledging the existing relations of force. So now, after 1922, the constantly changing relations in the Far East, rubbing against the objective of our waiting game, determined our Far Eastern policy. "China, Russia and Japan," continues Griswold, "furnished the factual substance with which that policy was obliged to deal. The rise of Chinese nationalism, the revival of Russian power and the advance of Japanese imperialism created practical problems demanding practical solutions. These were conflicting elements artificially frozen into the *status quo* of the Washington treaties. When they began, as it were, to thaw, to pass once more into change and motion, they presented a pragmatic challenge to all principles and doctrines."

We met the challenge by — appeasement. We wanted a Chinese government strong enough to put down native anti-imperialist movements but not to cast off our own controls. We feared the stimulating effect, not only on the Chinese but on all the colonial peoples, of the growing strength of the Soviet Union. We shaped our policy accordingly. Our vigorous effort to contain the Japanese in the days after War I, was abandoned and even reversed. Professor Taylor makes the comparison between the American attitude in the early 1920's and that of the 1930's.

In the 1920's, "at a time when the United States certainly had no love for the revolutionary government of Russia, which it did not even recognize until 1933," we launched the Siberian expedition, less to put down the Bolsheviks than "to see that Japanese troops returned to Japan. It was made perfectly clear to Tokyo that any attempt to take advantage of Russian weakness for purposes of territorial expansion in Siberia would be considered by the United States as an unfriendly action." But when Japan invaded China, we kept hands off.

"Why, then, did not the United States act with an equal vigor against Japan in 1931?" Why? Because the great private commercial and financial interests no longer minimized the strength of revolutionary Russia. They had been badly scared by the 1922-1927 period of the Chinese Revolution when it appeared that, with the moral backing and material aid of the Soviet Union, the Chinese would establish a "territorial and administrative integrity" independent not only of Japan and Britain, but of the United States as well. So, to our shame, we began to strengthen the Japanese, or at least, carefully refrained from interfering with her aggressions against China.

"The United States was not anxious to weaken Japan too much in relation to the Soviet Union, and there was always the hope that the two could be maneuvered into fighting each other as they had done in 1904-1905," Professor Taylor explains.

But that is the essence of the policy of appeasement as put into effect by the British in the dark days of Neville Chamberlain. The basis of Chamberlain's far-fetched scheme was the belief that Germany and Russia could be set fighting until they had bled themselves white, then Britain would be left the strong man of Europe.

In the Far East, the United States applied the appeasement principle from the middle of the 1920's. Russia was to be weakened even if it meant also weakening China; Japan was to be the means of bleeding Russia. That is why we sold scrap to Japan right up to the fall of Holland in 1940. Professor Taylor says:

"The stronger the Soviets became, the more reluctant were the Western Empires to weaken Japan by opposing her expansion." Moreover, everything seemed threatening to the imperialists. "There were riots in Java and Sumatra in 1926, signs of unrest in Burma." India was aflame. Later, Chinese resistance to Japan spurred the nationalism and the urge for liberty of all Asia, "making the great powers reluctant to enlist the help of their subjects against the menace of Japan for fear that these peoples might ultimately turn against their own rulers."

The Soviet Union, many have forgotten, was giving China arms to fight the Japanese despite the violently anti-Communist policy of Chiang Kai-shek. Our policy-makers, by a cold-blooded calculation, determined that it would suit our ultimate interest to let Russia expend arms and China bleed. Says Taylor: "Before the fall of Holland created a threat to United States interests in the south, our policy towards China [primarily sought] to keep both sides fighting in order that Japan should waste her strength against the Chinese. So long as the Soviet Union was supplying China with the bulk of its arms, and Japan was not threatening southeast Asia, there was no reason to stop the flow of [American] war materials to Japan."

The fall of Holland changed everything. Holland had a peculiar role in Europe and in Asia, "that of a weak power controlling very important strategic areas. No Great Power could permit another Great Power to control the wealth of the Indies; but Holland could be left in this position because she was not strong enough to oppose the general policies of the stronger empires." Japan was strong enough. Japanese rule would mean exclusion of British and American imperialists. The fall of Holland in Europe, therefore, threatening the fall of Holland in the Indies, forced a reversal of American policy in the Far East.

Thereafter, the great fear was that Japan would become too strong and emerge as the unchallengeable ruler of Eastern Asia, with ultimate power over India and Siberia. In the changed situation, a bid for American power could only take the form of direct aid and even intervention.

Hence China was included in the flow of lend-lease materials, an American military mission was established, and the hour of open warfare with Japan drew near. Pearl Harbor was a treachery but it was not a surprise.

So it was that appeasement failed in the Far East as in Europe. The fall of Holland showed that Britain had miscalculated the forces with which she was dealing in Europe; subsequent events showed we had underestimated the strength of Japan. Who knows how large a percentage of the American lives sacrified in the bitter Pacific war were an unnecessary sacrifice to the folly of appeasement, to the passion of anti-Communism, to the unspeakable secret desire to maintain the power of imperialism in the Far East?

THE RIPE APPLE

It must be said that American imperialist aims were not wholly submerged in the just war against the Axis, and this truth is most clearly observed in the Far East. President Roosevelt may have considered that in taking steps to oust the British, for instance, from their imperialist positions in China and elsewhere, he was hastening the end of reactionary colonialism. Yet he can hardly have been unaware that powerful American private and selfish interests were the immediate beneficiaries of such behind-the-guns diplomacy.

An example of how the United States utilized our major role in the Pacific war to destroy British imperial positions built up over the course of a century, is supplied by Elliott Roosevelt in his book, *As He Saw It* (the "he" being President Roosevelt). Elliott writes:

"I mentioned I had heard that all our air reconnaissance and aerial mapping of China was strictly withheld from British view."

Anyone even slightly acquainted with the diplomacy of power will recognize the meaning of the fact indicated here by Elliott Roosevelt. It signifies displacement of the British by the Americans in the tutelage of a weak and feudal Chinese regime. President Roosevelt replied:

"We worked out that arrangement with the Chinese quite some time ago. Chiang wants very badly to get our support to keep the British from moving back into Hong Kong and Canton . . . We will support his contention that the British and other nations no longer enjoy special empire rights in China."

It is not necessary to speculate on whether American advisers suggested to Chiang that he seek American "aid" in ousting the British. President Roosevelt himself made it clear that the United States was taking all the initiative in deciding the future relations of Britain and America to China. When Elliott suggested that Churchill might resist, he replied sharply:

"There can't be much argument, inasmuch as 99 per cent American material and American men are bringing about the defeat of Japan."

Elliott adds that, "Father and the Generalissimo had also talked about the Malay States, about Burma and Indo-China and India," and President Roosevelt had indicated what we would and would not permit after the war in all those areas.

All of this the British could do little to prevent — so long as preservation of their empire with all that imperialism implies, was the center of their policy. That is as true for a Labor as for a Tory government. Loss of control over the oceans symbolized loss of control over her own empire for such an imperial Britain; it spelled permanent dependence upon the United States for her continued pretense of major world rank. What Britain might still do by a revolutionary reversal of her regime and her economy, a definite abandonment of imperialist exploitation as the basis of her national life, is a matter for the conscience of the British people. An American observer can do no more than record the fact of Britain's displacement by the United States in various spheres of imperialist influence.*

It is more important for an American observer — considering the workings of our national system of self-deception — to record our present attempts to impose United States rule in the Far East. We may prefer to bury our heads in the sands of our own self-righteousness, but to all other eyes it is evident the United States asserts a claim to military-strategic domination of all China proper, half of Korea, and all of Japan. To all other understandings than ours, the United States is clearly committed to consolidating its hold on these regions and to keeping them permanently within its sphere of influence. Americans do not acknowledge this because, as will be seen later, we have an alibi.

---

* An American, Ernest T. Nash, who served for twenty-five years in the International Municipal Administration in Shanghai does record this phenomenon, and very emphatically at that. In a long letter to the Times (October 24, 1948), he refers to the "upsurge of United States dominance in China"—only to plead for careful study of British historic methods of maintaining our rule there! That gives all the more point to his blunt admission: "The entire map of China would today appear colored as an American 'sphere of influence' from which the British are excluded because of Britain's retreat following her European exertions."

A correspondent of the *Times* further underscores this point in a dispatch from London on January 12, 1949, just before the collapse of Chiang Kai Shek. The correspondent noted that the British government wanted a new joint Anglo-American policy to meet the wholly changed situation in China, but was unwilling to take any initiative because "Asiatic affairs north of Canton are, by rule of thumb, generally agreed to be the province of the United States in the diplomatic field."

CHAPTER 11

THE DAIREN ALIBI

The evidence of American expansion in Asia is so much on the surface, so little concealed, that one wonders how we succeed in ignoring what everyone else knows. But we do not really ignore it. On the contrary, the trick is to acknowledge the evidence but deny its meaning. Our expansion is not expansion at all; it is a great crusade to halt Soviet expansion. This has been dinned into us ever since the death of President Roosevelt. It is the excuse for everything we do. It is the special form of the "moral" argument that has crystallized in the Truman Doctrine.

The moral argument in its primitive form is standard diplomatic dressing for too naked self-interest. "The art of sugar-coating a policy by attempting to explain it upon the basis of fair play and international morality—is omnipresent in diplomacy," Professor Williams remarks. But the decking out of plain material gain in the fine feathers of morality does not long remain an innocent pastime. The moral argument has a dangerous sequel: it creates a villain to balance the hero-role we have assigned ourselves. As the other great power of today's world, Russia was the only possible candidate for the part.

With the parts assigned, the play begins. It might be called, "The Double Standard." The acquisition of bases by the United States six thousand miles from home, becomes a harmless idiosyncrasy when it is not a positive virtue. A security-base obtained or sought by the Soviet Union on her very borders is "Red Imperialism." If we make investments or loans and send missions to supervise expenditure of the money, missions with the power of veto over any act of the debtor government, that is described as "generous aid." And, in the words of Secretary Marshall, to call it "imperialist aims," or to say it is an attempt "to fasten upon the recipients some form of political and economic domination," is "fantastic misrepresentation" and "malicious distortion of the truth." Yet if Russia concludes what the newspapers have styled a "fifty-fifty" deal with a neighboring country, that is "economic hegemony" imposed upon an "unwilling victim."

This double-standard has been the stock-in-trade of almost all our opinion machinery and officials since the death of Mr. Roosevelt. Over and over they have repeated the iniquities of the Soviet Union and the duty of the United States to thrust its power all over the globe lest the Russians, in some unspecified way, get there first. When even so eminent a citizen as Henry Wallace, intimate collaborator of President Roosevelt, dared to dissent, he was first ousted from the Cabinet, next denied space in the press, and finally denounced as a "traitor."

Little by little this lynch-psychology has come to govern our conduct of foreign affairs, paralyzing, if it does not quite convince, the mass of American opinion. Spurious "moral" arguments, repeated day after day, have become a material force in world affairs. American and Russian operations beyond the borders of the two countries are seen as in Coney Island distorting mirrors. Every Soviet act is multi-magnified and warped beyond recognition. Every American act is softened in outline and reduced in extent. The double-standard has proved particularly effective in concealing the *relation* between American and Soviet positions or actions in the same region.

The famous Dairen Incident, whipped up into a nine-day wonder by the press, admirably illustrates not only this aspect of the double-standard but the broader process of manufacturing "public opinion" and carrying out foreign policy under its protection. A small American warcraft calling frequently at Dairen as a kind of courier for the American consul there, carried out its usual mission on a visit from December 18 to 20, 1946. It arrived carrying two newspapermen and an official of the great Rockefeller oil trust that rings the world. The three passengers knew they were not authorized to visit the area but took a chance on obtaining Russian permission on the spot. Permission was denied; they remained aboard the vessel while its regular business was transacted and left with the ship when it departed.

Upon his return to China proper, one of the newspapermen, William H. Newton of the Scripps-Howard press, filed a dispatch sensationalizing the colorless incident. Newton, incidentally, has specialized in lurid anti-Soviet stories of the kind sought particularly by his employer and by the Hearst papers. His account of the affair, duly headlined throughout the United States on December 23, 1946, was that the Russians had issued an "ultimatum" to the American vessel, the LC-3 1090, to get out of Dairen in twenty minutes — or else! The general effect of the press sensation and the tone of accompanying editorials, was of pretended mystification at Russian presence in Dairen and fury at Russian threats to Americans.

On the first count, a dispatch to the *Times* from Benjamin Welles in Peiping, under dateline of December 18, 1946,—*before* the visit—gives some ground for suspicion that Newton was sent to Dairen to cook up a scandal. Welles' message shows that "the controlled part of the Chinese press" was engaged in a concerted campaign to create just such an atmosphere as the "Dairen Incident" did whip up in the United States. And it must be remembered that the "Nationalists" controlling their press are under hour-to-hour influence of American advisors, with our bellicose Navy "diplomats" furnishing most of the advice.

In the Chinese press campaign, said Welles, "a basic fact in the situation is ignored. Under the terms of the Sino-Soviet agreement of August 14, 1945, the Soviet Union received from the Chinese government the right to assume full military protection of the Port Arthur military base area. This area, as defined by the signatories, includes not only the city of Dairen but also the whole tip of the Liaotung Peninsula south of a line drawn east of Chinchow."

The State Department at first took much the line of the Welles dispatch in dealing with the press uproar over the "incident." On December 24 it declared the Russians were within their rights in the matter. After a week of headlines, "a spokesman" for the department announced that official reports showed that there had not been "in any sense an ultimatum." On the contrary when the vessel's 48-hour regular clearance expired, a "Soviet official on the dock, on his own responsibility and without referring the question to higher authority, granted a 2-hour extension." Twenty minutes before the end of the two hours, the official reminded the ship's officers that he had acted on his own and if the vessel overstayed the two hours, he himself would be in line for whatever Soviet displeasure might be expressed. That was all there was to it.

But the powerful interests that make American policy, were not content to let the matter drop. Their pressures on the Administration, on Congress and on the State Department are reflected in the press handling of the "Incident," especially that of the *Times*. I repeatedly cite the *Times* because it not only devotes more space to foreign affairs but because it speaks for the real policy-makers.

It is interesting that the next newsbreak in the affair, the State Department's repudiation of the repeatedly headlined "ultimatum," was not even published as a separate story in the December 27 *Times*. It was buried on page six in a Washington dispatch on another matter. Four lines of heads above the story referred to the other matter. One line, "Dairen Aid Acknowledged," was the only clue to the buried story that the State Department denied there had been any "ultimatum." An editorial in the same issue of the *Times* showed that the burial was not accidental; it reflected disapproval by the *Times* and the all-powerful interests it represents, of State Department behavior. Said the editorial:

"Instead of patting the Dairen Russians on the back with the declaration that they were well within their rights in telling us to go to blazes, it seems to us that the State Department could properly address a courteous inquiry to Moscow, based on this incident, asking how soon Russia proposes to carry out the pledge of August 14, 1945, to respect Chinese authority in Manchuria 'as an integral part of China.' "

The secret pressures behind the *Times* public rebuke to the Department were wholly effective. The Department—the United States Government, with all that may mean in the way of effect on your life and mine—was forced to reverse its position. That same day, December 27, Under Secretary of State Dean Acheson announced that the Department had not, after all, reached any conclusion about the Dairen Incident. It was awaiting what a headline called "new Dairen data." The continuing pressure found open expression in another *Times* editorial on January 1, 1947. Replying to a *Pravda* article about the fake ultimatum the *Times* said:

"Dismiss the twenty-minute ultimatum. It wasn't the important point. The important point, thoroughly confirmed by *Pravda,* is that a Russian military commander at Dairen asserts the right to say what Americans may land and how long an American ship may stay in a friendly port of China. A dispatch yesterday from Nanking says that the Chinese government does not recognize Russia's right to continue occupying Dairen and is eager to take over the administration of that port . . . We think that our own State Department, instead of apologizing for the action of the Dairen Russians, would be better advised to help China achieve this proper and reasonable object."

On January 6, 1947, the State Department surrendered.

It announced that it had sent an official note to the Soviet and Chinese governments, and, while the note did not mention the "ultimatum" incident, it was cited to reporters as the *first official* statement of American policy since the incident. In other words, the earlier Department statements, including its rejection of the "ultimatum" story, were repudiated. The note said this government saw no reason "why there should be further delay in re-opening the port of Dairen, under Chinese administration." The note recognized that it was primarily a matter between China and Russia, but said unidentified "American interests" were affected. It hoped that "normal conditions" permitting "American citizens to visit and reside at Dairen in pursuit of their legitimate activities," might be established quickly.

The *Times* hailed this note—with an undertone of personal triumph — as "a significant return to the traditional American policy of the Open Door in China." The notes "intervene in the matter" not just to permit American interests to return to Dairen "but also elsewhere in Manchuria," exulted the editorial. But the meaning of "American interests" and of a century of Far East ambitions culminating in the "Open Door," is to be found nowhere in the columns about the Dairen Incident. The press and State Department alike forgot, throughout the affair, to mention the nature and extent of American expansion and ambitions concealed by the very hullaballoo about Dairen.

The vessel that called at Dairen on the famed visit, came from Tsingtao. Yet throughout the flurry not one of the publicists, business men and officials crying for Russian evacuation of Dairen, thought it necessary to ask what we are doing at Tsingtao. Two dispatches by Benjamin Welles six months later, nevertheless, show the inescapable connection between American positions at Tsingtao and the manufactured "incident" at Dairen. Needless to say, there have never been any page one headlines about Tsingtao; the *Times* one-column inside-page heads on the two Welles dispatches overflowed with honey: "Navy at Tsingtao a U. S.-China Bond," and "Tsingtao Friendly to U. S. 7th Fleet." Yet the content of the dispatches hardly justified the tone of the heads. The dispatches revealed, in effect, that our presence at Tsingtao was part of a plan involving the aid of the ruling clique of China, to make American power the dominant force in the Far East.

"Tsingtao is a paradox in United States-Chinese relations. Here, in China's finest anchorage Admiral Charles M. Cooke's powerful United States Seventh Fleet guards the western extension of American Pacific power. Here in sovereignty-conscious China, 'extra-territoriality' for Americans still exists in form if not in substance . . .

"This working cooperation in Tsingtao is not pure chance . . . China's leaders, shrewd realists, have long seen that Japan's defeat left a power vacuum in the Western Pacific. They have been anxious *and, more important, the United States government has been determined that this vacuum shall be filled by American naval strength* in preference to that of any other Pacific power."

All the fuss about Dairen then, adds up to the fact that the United States is determined to dominate the Far East. The technique of consolidating our naval rule involves the building up of Chinese naval forces in categories and craft completely dependent upon relations with the American Navy of which they are a mere auxiliary. Thus, as the dispatches say, 271 "surplus amphibious craft and landing craft have been turned over to the Chinese and the U. S. Navy is training Chinese crews.

"In view of the disturbed international relations in the Pacific, few Americans here expect the United States naval forces will depart from Tsingtao on completion of the naval training program in 1951."

Can any honest journalist conceal his blushes for the

Dairen furore and the smug State Department note of January 6, as he reads this? We haven't even contracted to get out before 1951 and don't intend to get out then! For "it does not take long for a visitor to Tsingtao to appreciate that the transfer of 271 small craft and the training of Chinese sailors are not the basic reasons for America's presence here. America's strategic needs in the Pacific Ocean and her attempts to stabilize the Far Eastern situation," i.e., to entrench American power, are the real reasons.

One might wonder how Russian war vessels would be received in Tsingtao if any were disposed to emulate the provocations of American "sailor diplomats." Our press does not tell us. Welles, noting that senior naval officers say Tsingtao is not a true "American naval base" because it would have to be evacuated for fear of air attack in the event of war, adds this significant comment: "But it is an inescapable fact that Tsingtao is only 190 miles south of Port Arthur, Russia's southern-most Pacific base. . . . The mere presence of American fleet units at Tsingtao can be said to satisfy our strategic needs in the Western Pacific but at the same time it complicates our political relationships with Russia in the Far East."

One may talk, as Welles does, in Truman Doctrine terms: "that America is determined to bar armed expansion into the western Pacific from the north," but the facts of his dispatches and of the Dairen incident itself show that the expansion is all ours. The Dairen furore, insofar as it was not a mere blind for Tsingtao and Tsingtao's wider implications, was *not* an attempt to halt a Soviet expansion effort. It was, even on its face, a demand for a Soviet retreat; it called upon the Russians to abandon a treaty-right flowing from pre-Soviet history, formally conceded by the United States and Great Britain in 1945 and thereupon confirmed by a Soviet-Chinese treaty.

A last word. The January 6, 1947 note and the press

headlines about the Dairen Incident, exploited public dislike of foreign domination over a *Chinese port*. From that point of view, Tsingtao is a lesson in hypocrisy. The American people, as little as they hear of Tsingtao, hear that little in terms of warm "Chinese cooperation." The Chinese press, however, constantly reports incidents, despite the censorship, that reveal an inner fury of resentment at American presence on Chinese soil. The resentment sometimes overflows into street demonstrations and is then reported here in distorted form. The real content of the matter is best revealed by an incident that was more worthy of headlines than the Dairen affair though it won just three tiny paragraphs in the *Times* on April 22, 1947.

The incident occurred in Tangku, a port of embarkation reserved for American use, civilian and military. American military police "insulted and threatened a group of Chinese reporters who were visiting the port of Tangku Sunday," the item revealed. "The Chinese reports said one Marine threatened to shoot anyone taking pictures and that he and another American forced the Chinese at gun-point to re-board their bus." Thus, while the Dairen headlines made much of supposed Russian arrogance *toward Americans* in a Chinese port, it is the *Chinese themselves* who are told where they may and where they may not go in American-occupied China!

CHINA, KOREA, JAPAN

This business of making ourselves at home in China—and making the Chinese subordinates in their own home—will not surprise those who have examined our present position in the Far East against the background of long imperialist intrigue. They will be prepared to find the United States now seeking to exercise that sole control which was the implicit purpose of a dozen strategies employed in the last fifty or even a hundred years. But they will be impressed by the increasingly military character of American expansionism in that part of the world.

The ruling caste of China, seeking backing against its own discontented population, has accepted economic, financial, and military tutelage, which is bound to add up to political control. It has not sought or obtained this tutelage from a combination of the powers, but from the United States alone. American military advisers, American arms, American instructors, American-directed expenditure of American loans — the realist will expect to find American participation in China's internal affairs.

Of course he will find it. A United States Military Advisory Group (Magic) has been growing steadily since it was set up in anticipation of Congressional authorization — which failed to arrive! It is said to number 3,000 officers and men. It recently agreed to undertake training, in Formosa, of ten combat divisions for use in Manchuria and North China. The Navy branch of Magic, aside from "training Chinese seamen" at Tsingtao, "assists" in operation of the Chinese Naval Academy at Shanghai. The air branch of the outfit has advisers at eleven schools according to dispatches in November 1947. All branches in fact have functions closely related to direct participation in combat.

The most competent observers not only fully document an account of American intervention in Chinese affairs, but describe that intervention as disastrous. Disastrous, that is, not merely to the peace of the world, not alone to the Chinese people in the path of the civil war encouraged by our intervention, but to the very forces we have attempted to strengthen by our aid. After a few boasts about quickly mopping up the Chinese Communists, the regime of dictator Chiang Kai-shek has admittedly gone into its worst crisis and the so-called Nationalist-ruled portion of China threatens to fall into anarchy.

It is not necessary to read the future. The present reality is enough: the United States is strategically in command of the whole of China proper, to whatever extent the completely dependent "Nationalist" government is in command of it. The shakiness of the Nanking regime should not cause us to ignore that the United States is, nevertheless, sufficiently in control of China proper to move in troops and set up air and naval bases at will. Whatever tomorrow may bring, that is the fact today.

This strategic colonization of China must be seen in the context of American military-strategic expansion throughout the Far East. Korea and Japan fill out the picture. If Tsingtao is only 190 miles from the Soviet outpost at Port Arthur, Korea's northern border touches Soviet soil within a few miles of Vladivostok, chief Soviet Pacific port. And neither our present behavior nor past history suggests that we have any intention of getting out of Korea.

The United States pried Korea open to Western trade in the early 1880's but it soon became the object of Japanese and Russian rivalry. It was one of the principal prizes sought by Japan when she made causeless war on China, nominal ruler of Korea, in 1894. Though China was powerless to deny Japan's demand at the 1895 peace settlement that she grant "independence" to Korea to cover Japanese seizure, Russia was not powerless. She organized a bloc of European empire-states in the Far East and forced Japan to get out. She herself moved in. At this point Japan, in no position to fight Russia, proposed a friendly division of the loot. *She suggested the partition of Korea at the 38th parallel,* the northern half to go to Russia, the southern half to herself. Russia refused, and less than ten years later Japan was able, with Anglo-American instigation and aid, to fight and defeat Russia and to take Korea. American capital shared in the exploitation of Korea though on increasingly inferior terms. With Japan now eliminated as an independent agent, the policies pursued by American occupation forces in southern Korea, seem to mark an intent to claim at least the former Japanese sphere permanently for the United States. The setting up of a Korean "government" by an American-controlled United Nations commission in the summer of 1948, was quickly followed by the announcement that the United States — not the United Nations — would train and arm Korean "security" forces under the new "independent" government.

As a matter of fact, dispatches in 1947 following United States rejection of a Soviet proposal for immediate withdrawal of all troops from Korea, reported even anti-Communist Koreans as increasingly cynical about the American role.

Another dispatch from Seoul during the same period, by Hearst correspondent Ray Richards, was more direct. It said "strategy officers in the American Army of Occupation in Korea" had demanded "a mighty base on the Korean island of Quelpart, known to the Japanese as Saishu and to the Koreans as Cheju." That proposal, it said, "is now embraced in the discussions of the Army and Navy Joint Planners at Washington."

Richards also quoted Kim Koo, Korean rightist leader, as promising that if he and his followers were installed in power in Korea, "one of our first moves would be to offer the United States military sites on Quelpart."

A controlled "Korean" government would be just one possible cover for continued American strategic control of the country. It might be done by facilitating Chinese control, that is control by dependent Chinese feudal forces. But such is the situation in China that all signs point to quite another solution: attempted ultimate restoration of Japanese domination, this time at the service of American private capital and United States strategic interests.

Such an American-controlled Japanese domination, not of Korea alone but of all China, is seriously feared in the latter country. On July 10, 1947, Dr. Fei Hsiao-tung, described by *Times* correspondent Tillman Durdin as an "eminent Chinese political analyst," and strongly pro-American, said the United States regarded "Nationalist" China as a weak and unreliable base for its strategy in the Far East. "The United States has already decided to shift her attention to Japan," with a view toward war with Russia, he declared. *Ta Kung Pao*, newspaper of the "political science clique" of the Kuomintang, makes the same complaint. Moreover, a poll conducted by the paper in May 1947, shows what the Chinese really consider to be the meaning of American policy in the Far East. In the poll:

1. A majority of the voters indicated their belief that Japan would again be the strongest power in the Far East in five years.

2. Six-sevenths of the persons polled believed Japan would eventually invade China again!

Throughout 1948, American policy brought public demonstrations of resentment in China. They grew in scope even after the American Ambassador, under the pretext of protesting to the Chinese Government against "anti-American" actions, had virtually demanded and procured police violence against the demonstrators.

It must be admitted that United States control of Japan is of a nature to encourage panic. We rule Japan absolutely, solely, and without recourse. American rule of Japan is declared to be only for the most selfless ends. Moral declarations are excellent—in church—but any group that has the responsibility of governing a nation can scarcely afford the luxury of taking such declarations at face value. Statesmen of all nations, whatever they may say in public, will state in their confidential reports that Japan must be regarded today as part of the military-strategic empire at the disposition of the United States. The country is patently intended to remain under permanent American control no matter what changes in the form of administration may take place.

CHAPTER 12

DOMINATION WITHOUT ANNEXATION

"American imperialism? Frankly, I think it's simply silly. I hope we shall wind up with a few new bases for our national defense. But everybody with a grain of sense, ought to know that we plan no conquests anywhere; that we ask only 'justice' and the 'open door' and 'democratic good will' and peace around the world."

The speaker was Senator Vandenberg. He had just returned from a Big Four conference — in 1946 when the Big Four were still conferring. American expansion? Nonsense! Without naming Henry Wallace, who had questioned the all-righteousness of American policy at about that time, Vandenberg hit out at him in these words:

"I confess I get weary of these libels — especially when uttered against us by our own domestic agitators."

How do they do it? How do our policy-makers dare to ignore the expansion described in detail in preceding chapters? How do they hope to persuade the people in the face of the record?

"The question as to why Americans believe these falsehoods is easily answered," Professor Frederick L. Schuman wrote in a review of former Secretary of State Byrnes' book, *Frankly Speaking*. "They have been assured of their truth by most of their newspapers and periodicals, by almost all commentators still broadcasting, by many of their clergymen, and by virtually all of their public leaders, including Mr. Byrnes."

But Byrnes and Vandenberg wouldn't dare if it weren't for the press. They know, however, that the press daily "proves" the official view of an expanding Russia and a contracting Anglo-America, by gathering and displaying news to fit the picture. It is not a matter of simple suppression; it is a subtle thing. The vast resources of the multi-billion-dollar news industry are employed to maintain a constant flow of stories purporting to show tireless Soviet activity abroad. Correspondents in Seoul, Vienna or the Antarctic know that any item about Russia is welcome. By a turn, a twist, an interpretation, a headline, these activities or imagined activities, become "evidence" of what is now called "the new Russian imperialism."

If the same resources were employed to describe the most important trend in world affairs today, stories of American pressures would pour in from fifty capitals each day, fighting one another for the headlines. They would tell, without previous doctoring, today's true history of human butchery by vicious regimes all over the world, under the direct pressure of American imperialism. But that's exactly what they don't do.

Let me cite a case. Gendarmes of the present American-sustained Greek government, having decapitated prisoners in their care, went on parade carrying their victims' heads on pikes. Had this happened in, say, Poland, it is not difficult to imagine the headlines here. But there were no headlines and as far as I know no stories until the London *Daily Mirror* published pictures of the grisly affair. That forced the British Foreign Office to make the diffident gesture of calling the Greek government's "attention" to the "reports." The British action finally got the story into print here. I found it in the New York *Herald-Tribune* as a 12-line item, between the radio column and the theater ads, under the "objective" one-column head, "To Question Greek 'Atrocities.'"

That kind of "balance" and "objectivity" in our press gives our statesmen the assurance to dismiss, without reply, any charge of American imperialism or expansionism. But let's get back to the speech of the Senator from Michigan, with which we began this chapter.

Senator Vandenberg compared "Russian expansion" of "more than 250,000 square miles," to "our kind of 'imperialism' that has just established the free and independent commonwealth of the Philippines—just as it established the free and independent Republic of Cuba in the aftermath of an earlier war."

The fraud of Philippine "liberation" cannot be passed unchallenged. For independence is not to be measured solely by formal sovereignty. And by the same token, annexation or dis-annexation alone does not determine the colonial enslavement of a country or its liberation. The Philippine Islands were seized by the United States as a base for conquest of empire in Asia and long employed to that end. The United States has just begun to consolidate such an empire. Does anyone suppose, amid the shower of self-congratulations at our magnanimity, that we are actually going to put the islands on their feet, economically and militarily, and say, "Now, go it alone?" Only the excessively naive or the excessively cynical would dare answer, "Yes."

High Commissioner Paul McNutt has already answered, "No." In an article in *Collier's* of July 6, 1946, he said rather plainly that the Philippines would have to play the role assigned to them in American strategic plans for the Manila-Tokyo-Shanghai "triangle." And these are plans for expansion, not plans for defense.

"We are already committed to the maintenance of naval and air bases in the islands," McNutt said. "These are not designed merely for the protection of the Philippines, nor even for the defense of the United States. These bases are expected to be secondary, supporting installations for supply, repair, and staging activities for all our armed forces in the Far East. . . . Committed as we are to long-time occupation of Japan, to a strong policy in Asia, the Philippines are destined to play a major role in our diplomacy in the Orient."

Philippine elections were conducted in the presence of American troops and returned a president, Manuel Roxas, who is completely dependent upon American support for his rule and possibly even his life. How dependent was indicated during subsequent base negotiations when, as a dispatch from Manila in February, 1947, put it, "the Americans startled the Filipinos by offering to withdraw all their forces." This offer by McNutt was recognized as a threat and "was rejected quickly by President Roxas and his chief negotiator, Foreign Secretary Elpidio Quirino. The interchange was credited with strengthening the American bargaining position."

Even so, popular hostility to American or any other foreign occupation, compelled McNutt to pare down United States demands. The final agreement, signed in March, provided only 23 of the 73 bases originally demanded and specifically prohibited bases in Manila or its environs, or active bases in other population centers. These concessions were facilitated by the fact that, as the *Times* editorialized, "the Philippines no longer have a very important place in the defensive alignment we are building in the Pacific." Or, to be more candid than the *Times*, because American military leaders have made *Japan* the chief United States military base in the Far East! But whether primary or not in American strategic plans, the Filipinos pay the price of American expansion. This Associated Press dispatch dated January 11, 1948, needs no comment:

"The Philippines government has purchased 2,000 homes and is evicting more than 10,000 persons from scattered areas around the Clark Field air base, seventy miles north of Manila, to fulfill its obligations under the bases treaty with the United States. The area . . . will be under United States control for ninety-nine years."

Roxas repaid his election debt by procuring amendment of the Philippine constitution to give American capital extraordinary rights in the new "independent" Republic. A letter to the *Times* printed on December 22, 1946, excellently describes this process of putting golden chains on Philippine freedom. "The vast majority of the American people know absolutely nothing of a matter which seriously threatens American prestige and moral standing in the Philippines. I refer to the so-called 'parity provision' of the Bell Trade Act, which governs Philippine-American commercial relations." The writer then quoted this provision, as now embedded in the Philippine Constitution: "The disposition, exploitation, development and utilization of all agricultural, timber and mineral lands of the public domain, waters, minerals, coal, petroleum and other natural resources of the Philippines, and the operation of public utilities, shall, if open to any person, be open to citizens of the United States and to all forms of business enterprise owned or controlled, directly or indirectly, by United States citizens."

Roxas' attempts to convince Filipinos that nothing had been given away by this provision, produced some tortured logic. "We do not propose to grant equal rights to American citizens in any sense of the word," he said. "What we propose to grant is special rights, the right of equal treatment with regard to development of natural resources and ownership of public utilities. That is a far cry from parity." What that means perhaps Mr. Roxas knows.

Parity or no, the provision means that the Philippine Republic is helpless against harmful encroachments by powerful American private capitalist interests. All small or industrially undeveloped countries know that they must protect their young industries; otherwise powerful competitors from the advanced countries will kill them. When Puerto Ricans attempted to set up a soap factory in the Island, the great mainland Colgate concern sold Palmolive soap at two to three cents a bar for a period long enough to bankrupt the Puerto Rican soap firm. Puerto Ricans also put a million dollars into a refinery on the Island, a logical industry since there is plenty of crude petroleum barely four hundred miles away at Aruba. The giant British and American oil interests sold gasoline in Puerto Rico at twelve and fourteen cents a gallon just long enough to ruin the native refiners. The undeveloped countries know all these tricks. At the International Trade Organization conference in Havana which ran from late 1947 into the new year, they firmly resisted attempts of the developed countries to force adoption of an international trade charter that would have barred defensive measures. The representatives of the small countries said they must have freedom to pass laws protecting home industry from the monopoly giants of the advanced countries. The Philippines have freedom to protect themselves from British, French, Dutch or any other foreign capitalists except the Americans. The "parity" provision therefore not only permits American interests to exploit the Islands at will, but it protects the American bankers from British or other competitors. With no competition, they can impose their own terms, exactly as they do in the helpless colonies.

Roxas was able to obtain ratification of these "special rights" or "equal rights" or American "parity" rights. By any other name, the Islands remain a semi-colony. In another respect, there is a repetition of history. To establish American rule in the Philippines at the turn of the century, we crushed a native revolutionary movement which sought the national independence and the personal liberties we affect to prize. We fought a counter-revolutionary war. Now, to re-establish our rule after the defeat of Japan, we have had to give arms to the very Filipinos who collaborated with the Japanese. These ex-collaborationists have given American capital the rights of a master, and they are butchering other Filipinos who did most of the fighting against the occupation but want something more than a change of masters. American troops have also taken part in the fighting, and it is still going on. The United States has, in effect, indicated that it will not tolerate Philippine resistance to American domination.

All this was readily foreseeable—and was foreseen. A

Briton, G. F. Hudson, described the direction of events in 1937. In *The Far East in World Politics,* he wrote: "The Philippines are to be given their 'independence' in ten years time, but it will be strange indeed if in ten years the Washington State Department cannot find a formula for preserving the substance of American power."

The State Department has indeed found such a formula and it includes a purely nominal independence for the Philippines, despite the boast of Senator Vandenberg. It is an independence conditioned on American bases, exclusive economic privileges and other limitations that we unhesitatingly describe as "imperialism" when some other power than the United States is the beneficiary.

The case is no better with Cuba. Senator Vandenberg ranked that country with the Philippines as an outstanding example of American altruism in foreign affairs. Yet in an earlier chapter, that very dangerous "domestic agitator," banker Thomas W. Lamont conceded that Cuba is something less than "independent" as a result of American controls. The Cuban trade unions, during 1947, ran advertisements in American newspapers, highlighting the dependence of Cuba on decisions of the American government. The ads appealed to the American people to lend their "authority and influence to support a larger sugar quota for Cuba in the American market." The ads revealed how the men in Washington can move a decimal point and bring any Cuban government to crisis!

"For Cuba, with her colonial economy which depends solely on her sugar and tobacco exports," the ad ran, "a reduction of her quota of sugar for the American market will mean reducing her production, and, consequently, unemployment, poverty and hunger among the workers and farmers . . . When Cuban sugar revenue from the American market was curtailed as a result of the Smoot-Hawley Tariff Law . . . wages dropped to as low as 20 cents a day."

This "colonial economy" is the result of American domination of Cuba imposed by force of arms following the war with Spain; it gives the United States a decisive weapon to use against any Cuban government that might show signs of resisting American demands. The Cuban Sugar Act of 1947 was phrased to permit the United States to police Cuban payment of private loans to that country, to the great distaste of Cuba. It is obvious, therefore, that Senator Vandenberg can speak with such assurance only by ignoring the content of Cuban "independence." "Independent" Cuba was as tightly controlled by the United States from the time of the "liberation" as were the annexed Philippine Islands. The dis-annexed Philippine Islands are today as firmly a part of the American empire as they were prior to their independence. Senator Vandenberg, however, is making his own narrow definition of imperialism when he so easily rejects the charge against us.

Nor is it Senator Vandenberg's definition alone. There is no doubt that the chief argument on which the uniform denial of American imperialism rests, depends upon identifying "imperialism" with "annexationism." The United States, it is argued, is not imperialist because it generally avoids annexation of territory. There have been exceptions, such as Hawaii and the Philippines, but even in the latter case, "See, we have dropped our title," they cry. "We have a colonial empire, true, but on the whole we are not adding to our formal possessions." By thus concentrating our attention on the open and formal seizure of territory, ignoring the wide variety of forms under which an advanced nation may rule a "backward" one, we are able to convince ourselves of our own purity as compared to Russia's wickedness. The theme as formulated below by the *Times* (June 17, 1946), has been repeated almost word for word by Secretary Marshall and other high officials.

"That Russia has pursued a policy of unilateral aggrandizement in violation of the Atlantic Charter is no longer subject to debate . . . She has already annexed more than a quarter of a million square miles of territory, with some twenty-four million people, and has prompted her Polish satellite to annex the German territories put under its administration, with the city of Stettin thrown in as extra booty . . . In contrast, neither the United States nor Great Britain can be charged with aggrandizement. They have annexed nothing."

This pretense that imperialism is a synonym for "annexation," may or may not retain its hold on American public opinion for a long time to come. But it has very little effect, even now, on world opinion. The inhabitants of the scores of countries where we have "a few bases for our national defense" or veiled bases for some other purpose, are not to be taken in by self-righteous propaganda. In general, this theory of the identity of annexation and imperialism, can obtain only where there is ignorance of the facts of world-life. The peoples of Europe and Asia may be less literate than we; they may not receive the volume of news bulletins that we consume; but they generally have some knowledge of the history of imperialism. That has never been a popular study with us, but they did not have to study — they learned from the scars on their own hide, as the Spaniards say.

Their scars have taught them that absolute political dominance and unlimited economic exploitation are the fruits of imperialism, but that annexation is not its only form. There is no automatic danger signal to warn a nation at just what point foreign penetration threatens its real independence. There is no exact line determining the end of true sovereignty and the beginning of veiled dependency, nor is there always a great distinction between dependency and colony.

A Senate report on Hawaii just before annexation, explained: "Hawaii has been all the time under a virtual suzerainty of the United States, which is, by an apt and familiar definition, a paramount authority, not in any sense an actual sovereignty, but a *de facto* supremacy over the country."

In his classic, *Imperialism: A Study,* J. A. Hobson points out what he calls "the sliding scale of diplomatic language," using the terms "hinterland, sphere of interest, sphere of influence, paramountcy, suzerainty, protectorate, veiled or open, leading up to acts of seizure or annexation." And hypocrisy is not necessarily abandoned when annexation takes place. The seizure may be hidden under the form of "lease or leasehold," "rectification of frontier," a "concession," or, nowadays, a "trusteeship" replacing a World War I "mandate." And even before any of this diplomatic doubletalk has set in, a country or island or whole region may have fallen, for all practical purposes, into the position of a colony of a great power.

The need for some form of diplomatic title, and especially for annexation, only arises when the continued domination of some area by one Great Power is threatened by another. Hobson points out that Great Britain was "anti-imperialist" up to about 1870, that is, anti-annexationist, because she had a virtual monopoly of colonial imperial power. Only when other powers began to threaten her monopoly, did she feel the need of formally annexing the areas previously dominated and exploited by other forms. When rivals were about, she began to take territory if only to keep them from obtaining strategic positions from which to contest her domination of whole continents. That started the great territorial grab of 1870 to 1900 in which Africa and most of the remainder of Asia were parcelled out among the Great Powers.

The United States, too, had been "anti-imperialist" (that is, against annexation as the right form for domination and exploitation) up to that point. It is significant that such super capitalists as Andrew Carnegie were leaders of the "anti-imperialist" movement; just so, it was Benjamin Disraeli in England and Bismarck in Germany who first opposed "imperialism" (i. e., the wave of annexations) and then took the lead in the grab. When the United States saw the exploitable lands of the earth passing out of reach at the close of the nineteenth century, it also entered the race. Provoking war with Spain, we were able to seize that enfeebled power's choicest imperial possessions.

The average intelligent and informed American has been under no compulsion to understand these things. People elsewhere have; they were parts of the imperial process whether on the exploiting or the exploited end. But America's sudden open assumption of a world role must force Americans, too, to give up empty moral formulas for the hardboiled facts of economic, financial, diplomatic and military history.

In 1926 the *Times*, that great defender of the faith, could dismiss charges of imperialism against America on the ground that no one ever heard of an imperialist power without a great standing Army and Navy. Now we have the world's most elaborate military establishment, so our apologists have found a new alibi. The current way of pooh-poohing criticism is to point out that we are not making but losing money on our new Pacific islands (or even on Korea, Germany and Japan.) Secretary of the Navy Forrestal, in September, 1946, made this point while defending naval rule over the captured Japanese islands as well as over Guam and American Samoa. Citing a speech by ex-President Herbert Hoover who urged that the United States hold on to all the islands of the Pacific, Forrestal agreed with Hoover's contention "that such holding could not be held an extension of imperialism because we have no designs for exploitation."

Now this is interesting as an admission that not annexation but domination for the purposes of exploitation, is the test of imperialism. But it is naive in that it attempts to make the test on the basis of each island or region separately. Modern imperialism tends toward world rule, and any given territory may have great value as a strategic position even though it has no economic value in itself. Every colonial power has maintained costly and losing establishments as a part of its general power-structure. From the islands of the Pacific, domination of the rich resources of Asia may be gained, so a loss on those islands is no loss at all. It is typical of modern imperialism, moreover, that more territory is seized to keep it from rivals than is taken for its direct value, even for strategic purposes, to the power claiming ownership. Thus it will be recalled that the Navy's projects for the Pacific, as outlined by Struve Hensel in 1945, called for a limited number of bases but asked that the United States retain "hundreds" of islands to prevent their falling into other hands.

To some extent we Americans recognize and acknowledge this more subtle form of imperialism than the narrow annexationist formula of our main argument. We recognize and acknowledge it — in others. Thus Secretary Marshall, in a speech on July 1, 1947, coupled a denial of American "infiltration" with implicit accusations against Russia.

"There could be no more fantastic misrepresentation, no more malicious distortion of the truth than the frequent propaganda assertions or implications that the United States has imperialist aims or that American aid has been offered in order to fasten upon the recipients some form of political and economic domination," he said.

"No political parties subservient to United States interests have been left behind in European countries to attempt conquest of governments from within. No American agents have sought to dominate the police establishment of European countries. No 'joint American-European' companies have been forced upon reluctant governments."

Even in a literal and narrow construction, Marshall's words will not stand up against the facts. Political parties subservient to the United States government and perhaps to United States private interests have been established in governmental power in France and Italy as well as Greece, to name only the best-known cases. If these are not "reluctant governments," they are at least dependent ones.

Then, too, we "left behind" us, all over the world, American troops and ships at long-term land, air and naval bases, which also serve as bases for the penetration of profit-seeking American business interests. Paul V. McNutt, our ex-ruler of the Philippines, boasted of that recently. As summarized by the *Times* (January 30, 1948), he said: "Defense bases in the Far East, negotiated under 100-year treaties, now make it possible for the United States, through business groups, to build up the economy of the Orient." Bases and business — the imperialist twins.

And in that sense, Marshall's denials are at variance with the whole story of imperialism in our time and of American imperialism in particular. The typical twentieth century form of empire is economic penetration crystallized in financial control. It is a subtle and semi-invisible form of rule. In the nineteenth century, partition of continents, division of countries among rival powers by open or secret treaty (as Africa was divided and redivided between 1870 and 1900), closed spheres (as in China), were the characteristic forms of imperialism. But *the hidden exploitation of whole national and continental economies by one power — the United States — is the typical twentieth century form of imperialism.* And since technology has made the world smaller, the American supremacy in telecommunications, aviation, shipping — three national-interest-serving "private industries" which are worldwide by nature — gives American ambition a fillip. It reinforces the drive to extend this hidden exploitation until it has made the whole world one colony of American Big Business.

The drive for empire, however, centers on the struggle for world power. The invisible threads of dollar diplomacy meet at highly visible American bases. Dollar diplomacy, indeed, yields to atomic diplomacy. American private interests are secured in power by direct establishment of United States air, naval, land, weather and communications positions. These in turn top a structure built by indirect control of the military resources of two-thirds of the world through military missions, arms standardization, unequal alliances and maintenance of unpopular regimes which must be loyal to the United States because they depend upon American aid for survival.*

* President Truman's inaugural address contains the whole sequence. He makes the familiar disavowals: we want no territory or "privileges." Even when urging that we "foster capital investment" in backward areas by giving "guarantees to investors," he assures us it's an unselfish scheme: "The old imperialism—exploitation for foreign profit—has no place in our plans." But Washington comment on these passages (James Reston, *Times,* January 21, 1949) notes that the United States is increasingly interested in colonial strategic materials—copper in Northern Rhodesia, for instance—which are certainly produced under the most inhuman conditions of imperialist exploitation. The success of the whole anti-Communist "defense" plan advanced in the inaugural address, moreover, requires the continued subordination of the colonial continents to the advanced industrial powers. As Cyrus Sulzberger wrote from Geneva (*Times,* January 11, 1949): "If France, the Netherlands and Belgium were suddenly restricted to their continental territory (or Britain to the United Kingdom and the Dominions), the Marshall Plan would swiftly end in failure." To increase the exploitation of the colonies and to keep them in subjection, requires police power and bases. Hence Reston notes, in the dispatch above: "It is known that . . . the Ango-American combined Chiefs of Staff have shown considerable interest in the development of routes from East to West across Central Africa; that a supply base exists at MacKinnon, and that for economic, strategic and political reasons the British have been showing great interest in the development of East Africa."

CHAPTER 13

AMERICAN INFILTRATION

The Greek Government, midwife of the Truman Doctrine, is just such a government as our bankers and generals require for the purpose of legalizing the penetration of American interests. A minority regime which could not survive against popular resistance without the aid of American arms and money, it is absolutely subservient to the United States and, in fact, more and more yields its functions to the United States mission to Greece. A United Press dispatch from Athens, obviously based on information from the American officials in charge of United States aid, reported on June 16, 1947, that Americans had been assigned to all "Greek ministries to see where 'every dollar' of the $300,000,000 American grant goes. . . . American sources said the terms were 'tough' and paid only lip service to Greek sovereignty. Observers believed any powers given to Greece over control of expenditures from the funds would be little more than face-saving measures."

To what humiliating dependence the Greek government was reduced, was revealed in a dispute over the rights of American newspapermen. Foreign Minister Constantine Tsaldaris objected that the wording of a press clause in the agreement being negotiated with the United States, would "have my ministries full of American reporters going through the files." But, says the dispatch, "Mr. [Lincoln] MacVeagh [American Ambassador] flatly rejected any restrictions." He told Tsaldaris he "could complain about specific cases through the proper channels." Tsaldaris was forced to swallow this.

Thousands of specific incidents and hundreds of complaints in the Greek press were cited during United Nations debate on the Greek question from September to November, 1947, to back the Slav contention that the United States ruled Greece as a metropolitan country rules a colony. Or that we "put our feet on the table" as if we were "in our own house," to word it as Slav spokesmen often did. American representatives flatly declined to reply to these charges. Sure of a majority vote, they and their supporters argued that "the tattered clippings" only proved there was "freedom of the press," hence "democracy," in Greece. But as Dr. Ales Bebler, Yugoslav delegate retorted, the complaints cited were not from the opposition press; for the most part they came from the government parties and even from the newspaper of Tsaldaris, the "strong man" of the government. One such complaint was that Cabinet Ministers had to run to the American Embassy "a dozen times a day" during a Cabinet crisis because nothing could be decided without approval of the Americans.

Dispatches from Athens thereafter revealed that this kind of errand-boy government persisted. A UP wire on January 9, 1948 reported that Premier Sophoulis was "scheduled to reply to a memorandum by Dwight P. Griswold, chief of the United States mission," and would resign — together with Tsaldaris — if Griswold would not permit certain action in the money market. The crisis was averted, however, because the memorandum, as it turned out, approved the proposed action "in principle." It merely "insisted that in each case the United States mission must be consulted."

If this is not domination, what is it? From Paris to Shanghai it is seen for what it is; in fact, such absorption of Greece by the United States was predicted the moment the Truman Doctrine was proclaimed on March 12, 1947. Only in the United States do we persist in an attitude of innocence. "Poor Greece!" cried the *Ta Kung Pao,* leading newspaper of China, as Truman spoke. And from Paris four days after Mr. Truman's speech, rabidly anti-Communist *Times* man Harold Callender sent this dispatch:

"To a striking extent professional diplomatic quarters,

and other non-Communist or anti-Communist quarters, echoed in an only slightly attenuated form the Moscow charge of a new and expanding American imperialism. One of the first comments made by one of the leading diplomatic minds of Europe as he finished reading President Truman's message was that the President was pretty rough on Greece and Turkey.

"He was referring to President Truman's request to Congress to authorize the sending of American civilian and military missions to those countries 'to supervise the use of such financial and material assistance as may be furnished.'

"Among these seasoned if perhaps cynical experts in foreign relations there is apprehension that United States protection for Greece and Turkey in the form proposed by President Truman may lead easily . . . to something not far from United States protectorates over those countries."

These "seasoned" experts, of course, as the same correspondent elsewhere noted, cannot be persuaded that we are not directly interfering with democratic processes in France and Italy when we offer loans to regimes in those countries on condition that they exclude the Communist and Left Socialist parties, the parties with the largest popular following.

The least literate South American, Asiatic or European sees that the United States is infiltrating scores of countries in one form or another. Informed people outside the United States note that our overwhelming financial position is today employed in loans not only "supervised" by Americans but followed by military missions. The American intervention is so unpopular in Turkey that newspapers barely mention the proposed "aid" and "when they do they always carefully avoid mentioning any kind of American supervision in Turkey," a dispatch from Turkey said. From South America comes word that "Washington's hemisphere defense plan is looked upon with widespread suspicion."

Correspondent Frank Kluckhohn says "leaders of several countries have told this correspondent recently that in its present form it would be hard to swallow and almost certainly would not be digested in some key countries. There are a number of reasons for this. A basic one is the latent fear of United States 'imperialism.' "

Even the singularly corrupt feudal lords who rule in Latin America with the aid of American arms — "in the past several years at least four military revolutions have been fought with United States lend-lease arms" — and suck fantastic fortunes from their literally enslaved peoples, dread *Yanqui imperialismo*. Why not? "If all the Latin-American nations become exclusively dependent upon the United States for arms, the United States could decide whom to make strong and whom weak." The feudal generals of Brazil fear those of Argentina and vice versa.

Thus, though our press and radio work overtime to convince us of the "Russian menace," we ourselves are the menace feared by people in every quarter of the globe. On July 5, 1947, Miss Ruth I. Seabury, educational secretary of the American Board of Foreign Missions, said exactly that in an address before the New York Institute of International Relations at Colgate University.

"It may be hard to believe, but the United States, not Russia, is the number one fear of much of the world today," she declared.

The evidence comes from too many and too varied sources to be dismissed as "Communist propaganda." "A decent respect for the opinions of mankind" would in itself warrant our altering our course, but in truth there is something more than opinions to be heeded. There are facts. The facts show American infiltration everywhere. And precisely in the region of the Eastern Mediterranean, where the unsupported charge of threatened Russian expansion was used to justify the launching of the Truman Doctrine, the facts add up to unassailable proof.

The facts on one form of American infiltration — oil infiltration — provide as good an illustration of the general process as could be desired. The facts happen to be available for two main reasons. First, there is a leakage resulting from a many-sided tussle going on at this very moment as American influence is consolidated over the whole Near and Middle East. Second, the oil of Arabia, the central prize of this tussle, has provoked two law suits. Out of the lawsuits have come some interesting details which would normally have remained concealed for a quarter of a century.

The target of both suits is the American oil companies, which hold oil concessions controlling the entire reserves of Saudi Arabia, concessions captured under cover of the war. French interests backed by the French government, demanded a cut of this new booty in one suit. In the other, a retired American oil executive, J. A. Moffett, allegedly short-changed for his services to the American companies in the Arabian deal, seemed to want either to be paid off or to get revenge, so he talked pretty freely before the Senate War Investigating Committee and in court. Finally, the companies have released a good deal of information by way of beating both these opponents to the punch, that is, to take the sting out of any secrets they might reveal.

From all these sources, there emerges an unlovely picture of oil imperialism, with private interests and the United States government in the thick of it. These are the highlights: World War I eliminated German and Turkish interests from the Mediterranean-Near Eastern scene. An international grouping reflecting the War I alliance — Britain, the United States, the Netherlands and France — took over the oil of the region, with the British easily dominant. In the 1920's, the group greatly extended its operations by an "agreement" with the Iraq government. The easily-controlled Iraq government would have granted the concessions at an earlier date, if that were all there were to it; but the real importance of the agreement was that it marked acceptance by the various powers of percentages in accordance with their effective strength in the area. The terms of the agreement among themselves, however, included a provision that any additional oil rights acquired by one partner anywhere in the former Turkish Empire, should be for the account of all the partners.

There the matter stood until War II. Each partner, as is the way of imperialism, finagled for advantages contrary to the spirit of the truce, during the between-wars years. Standard Oil of California and the Texas Company acquired some concessions in Saudi Arabia. But they would never have been able to work the concessions if the relative strengths of Great Britain and the United States had remained unchanged. The outbreak of the war automatically revealed that those relations had really changed long ago. Britain was at once too involved in merely preserving her national independence from Germany to be able to protect her imperialist acquisitions of an earlier day. The United States moved in on Saudi Arabia and marked the whole Arabian peninsula for her own. American concessions covering a territory greater than the area of Texas plus California, were obtained.

That is the meaning of the more careful language of J. H. Carmical, *Times* business writer, telling the story from oil company sources: "When it was called to the attention of Washington in 1940 that the American companies might have difficulty in holding the Arabian concession, President Roosevelt gave the matter personal consideration. In supplying the Saudi Arabian government indirectly through the British with lend-lease funds, the President cautioned the Saudi Arabian Government about becoming involved in international politics and told the oil companies to let him know if at any time they encountered difficulties in holding the concession."

It was not just the financial resources of the United States that compelled Saudi Arabia to accept American dictation and compelled Britain to give up her predominance. It was the military power of the United States, made effective in the region by the wartime "ten front" policy of the United States and preserved today by, among other things, a base at Dhahran on the Persian Gulf. Though the British resent United States assumption of a "God-given right to go on consuming two-thirds of the world's oil stocks," and the French are suing for a share in the Arabian contracts, both countries know they will have to take what they can get. For the relations of force have changed.

"For years it has been recognized," writes Carmical, "that once British soldiers left the area it would be difficult for the present owners of the concessions to hold them. In fact, when the Iraq concession was obtained around 1925 by the international group, the head of one of the participating companies said that it could be held only so long as British soldiers remained." Now American "troops," in the more modern form of naval display, airmen, special advisors, and loans-with-strings to both Britain and Ibn Saud, hold the concessions. The British are allowed to remain and train a small army for Ibn Saud, for the benefit of the common account. Since the French are also well aware that the concessions rest on military force, "it is considered likely that the differences with the French will be dissolved without much difficulty and that the plans for the development and distribution of Middle East oil will go through as presently outlined. . . . The present plans, tacitly, at least, have the approval of Washington."

It is much more than tacit. The military-strategic interest claimed by the United States in the region is inseparable from the profit-interest of the private companies. As Clifton Daniel wrote in March, 1947: "Although the Arabian concession is obviously vital to us, the American government euphemistically maintains that it is purely a private, commercial operation. The French have not forgotten, however, that it was strong and persistent government intervention that obtained the first Middle Eastern oil rights for American interests in Iraq in 1927."

Daniel might have said, further, that our government pretends the matter is purely private only now that the oil companies are completely in the saddle and the Roosevelt influence has been eliminated. For under President Roosevelt, the government fought a hard but uphill struggle to keep the American interest a national and governmental one. Unfortunately, the nature of the struggle itself reveals how decisive, in a country like ours, is the power of the great Wall Street barons. Even with Mr. Roosevelt at the helm of the ship of state, they were too strong to tolerate any interference. In fact, the President was surrounded, in connection with the Arabian affair, with oil men in uniform. As Mr. Moffett publicly charged:

"In this connection it is both striking and I think significant, that former Army and Navy officers who, while in uniform, were in a position to affect government policies in connection with Arabian-American Oil Company dealings, are now holding important and lucrative positions with subsidiaries and affiliates of the Standard Oil Company of California and the Texas Company, joint owners of the Arabian-American Oil Company."

To name names: Admiral A. F. Carter. Moffett pointed out that before the war Carter was president of Shell Eastern Petroleum Corporation; during the war he was director of the Army-Navy Petroleum Board; he is now president of the Overseas Tankship Corporation, owned by the same companies that own Arabian-American.

The needs of the war did not bother these gentlemen. "The first move on the part of Washington," Carmical records, "included the proposal in 1943 that holders of the Arabian concession sell it to the United States Government. This they refused to do, and finally an effort was made to acquire an interest. This proposal also was rejected, and the next step by Washington was the suggestion that the

United States Government build a pipeline across Arabia to the Mediterranean Sea. However, this met so much opposition from the oil industry here that the pipeline as a government project also was dropped."

In short, the oil companies would not permit the government to have any voice whatsoever in the matter. The government must pay all the bills — you and I must pay them — but must not see or control what goes on between the companies and foreign governments and peoples. And the companies have had their way.

"At present," Carmical continues, "the plans for the development of the Middle East oil resources are being carried out without change except that the United States Government is not directly interested financially in the project."

The plans, as we shall see, go far beyond Saudi Arabia. Incidentally, Raymond Daniell in a *Times* dispatch from London on December 13, 1947, suggested that Mr. Truman is the man who finally swung the balance in favor of unrestricted oil-company control of these empire-size schemes.

"It was not until February 16, 1944, that the aspirations of private capital received the impetus of Government support," is Daniell's phrasing. "On that date Mr. Truman, as chairman of a Senate committee, recommended that the United States go into the Middle East on a large scale to replenish the oil reserves depleted by wartime demands of the armed services and our Allies."

(Oh, yes, the depletion argument. In 1947, the oil companies, despite vast foreign acquisitions, pumped up and sold more American oil than at wartime peak! Crude oil production averaged some 5,240,000 barrels daily against a top wartime level of 4,944,250 barrels registered one week in July, 1945. The truth is the companies want to produce and sell all the oil they possibly can here and throughout the world. Why not? With no price control, they had pushed the price up from $1.25 a barrel on March 31, 1946 to $2.65 at the end of 1947, a price increase that swelled their revenue by $2,600,000,000 a year according to the *Times* of January 2, 1948.)

This story means, in the first place, that every cent spent to secure concessions for the benefit of the private oil companies, has been paid by the American people, not by the companies. As Clifton Daniel writes, Arabian oil means "first, a supply for foreign markets of American companies — the opportunity to make money." Standard Oil of New Jersey and Socony-Vacuum are the leading distributors of oil in Europe, which is the natural market for Middle East oil. In addition to the 40 percent interest of these two companies in the Arabian-American Company, they buy a large part of the output of the British companies in Iran and Kuwait. The Rockefeller and Mellon interests have been handed a golden gift. As Moffett has testified without contradiction:

"The taxpayers paid for all improvements and investments and they (the oil companies) are sitting there with concessions worth billions of dollars, free and clear."

Not only did we pay for the concessions, but it often turns out that the huge profits made by these companies on investments they didn't make, are beyond the reach of taxation. Senate investigators discovered, for example, that Caltex (S. O. of Cal., — Texas Oil Co.,) incorporated in the Bahamas, made a tax-free $25,000,000 on a supposed investment of $1,000,000. A bagatelle. The Bahrein (Persian Gulf) Petroleum Company, incorporated in Canada, on an "investment" of $100,000 made — $92,000,000! Tax-free, of course.

A spade should be called a spade and a swindle a swindle. Such loot is the product of intrigues by the oil interests from positions inside the government. The Senate investigators found Max W. Thornburg, while in an $8,000-a-year post as Under-Secretary of State in wartime, was on the payroll of Standard Oil of California for $29,000-a-year. His letters to his employer, read into the record, indicated clearly that Arabian problems reaching him in his governmental capacity, were solved from an oil-company point of view. Thus he wrote to the company suggesting opposition to a proposed American agricultural mission to Arabia and to its suggested head, because "I don't see any good coming out of getting another man into our part of the picture. And, of course, his interests are not ours."

If these great gamblers stole nothing but our money, it might be permissible to tolerate their activities. But our peace and our lives are in their hands. For the effect of their victory for "private enterprise," their elimination of any governmental control over their operations, amounts to taking into their own hands the power of war and peace. If the people of the Arab lands revolt against corrupt rulers who give away their wealth, American force will be called on to "protect our interests." As Clifton Daniel remarked of the $100,000,000 project for a pipeline to carry the Arabian oil to the Mediterranean coast: "Protection of that investment and the military and economic security that it represents inevitably will become one of the prime objectives of American foreign policy in this area."

Honest men who think that the oil men, however big their profits, are really serving the interests of the United States, should sit in on the Senate investigation. Evidence heard there demonstrated that they "played both sides of the street" (as Harold L. Ickes, wartime Petroleum Administrator, put it). A letter on August 13, 1940 from Moffett, then in the employ of the companies, to H. D. Collier, president of Standard Oil of California, perfectly illustrates this ability to be on both sides simultaneously so long as there was a profit to be made both ways.

"You are doing a very large business with the Japanese and therefore must take as strong a pro-Japanese position as possible," Moffett wrote. But Standard's own Caltex (i.e., the Standard Oil-Texas Company subsidiary that first held the Arabian oil concessions later turned over to Arabian-

American Oil Co.), must follow an exactly opposite course, he said. This was because "we have a large investment in China, do a large business directly with China and practically nothing in Japan, and our main business is in the British Empire, which is having real difficulties with the Japanese and must be anti-Japanese at the present time."

At the direction of and for the benefit of a few men who control our big oil companies, and a few bankers involved in the loans and development projects, we have now achieved American supremacy throughout Arabia. As Paul P. Kennedy wired to the *Times* from Washington on July 3, 1947: "The program of increasing United States influence on the Saudi Arabian peninsula is gaining more than considerable momentum, it is believed in official circles here." He was referring to the visit of Prince Abdullah, son of Imam Yahya, first official of Yemen to visit the United States. Control of Yemen seals the position already attained in Ibn Saud's larger Arabian realm. Washington fully understood that the visit meant Yemen was leaving the British fold and entering that of the United States. Or, as Kennedy phrased it, rejecting [non-existent] "Russian and British influence in favor of the United States." The visit coincided "with reports that negotiations between the Saudi Arabian government and American interests for a private loan are reaching an advanced stage." Thus, all evidence points to a conviction in Washington that Arabia has been signed, sealed and delivered.

But if this does not constitute "imperialism" to our apologists, let us ask a question: what is the loan to Ibn Saud to be used for? The answer is, above all, a railroad from Riyadh through Hofuf to Dhahran. And who needs that railroad and for what purpose? Ah, there lies the secret of imperialism! Ibn Saud needs that railroad so that he can maintain his unpopular rule over the rebellious majority of Arabians and continue giving away the country's oil wealth in return for royalties that go into his own pocket and the pockets of his retainers. As Daniel cabled from Dhahran on January 26, 1947:

"The King is said to be insistent on the railway partly because, having conquered Saudi Arabia only twenty-five years ago, he wants to improve communications as a measure for keeping the country fully under control. The King knows . . . he could not defend Saudi Arabia against a major foreign invasion . . . but he seeks internal security."

We give him his railroad and by our position indicate that he can count on our support against rebellion; we permit a British military mission to be installed "to train and equip a small modern force," and thus we provide the profits Rockefeller's Standard Oil of New Jersey and the Mellon-owned Socony-Vacuum obtain from European sales of Arabian oil. But in the meantime, we enable Ibn Saud to oppress his people and we enable the oil men — we assist them — to contract obligations that the American people may have to discharge in person and arms in hand. We give over to them the conduct of our foreign policy in the Eastern Mediterranean. The Truman Doctrine follows where Rockefeller and Mellon lead. The red herring odor cannot overcome the smell of crude petroleum.

And still this is not the end. From our powerful military, economic and political base in Arabia, we send out lines of influence, that take in Trans-Jordan, Syria and Lebanon, to name only those countries caught up in the pipeline trail from Arabia. The choice of a route for a pipeline was political rather than economic; in fact, the decision to lay a pipeline was political. As Daniel wrote on March 1, "Laying down a pipeline, one of the world's largest and longest (1,100 miles of 30-inch pipe), will also mean laying down another major American interest in the Middle East parallel to that of Britain." Thus we prevent any British comeback to power in the region, forcing her to merge her interests with ours, under our direction. She cannot afford an oil war with us. She has, in fact, accepted her junior position; British companies are now planning construction, jointly with the Americans of some four other pipelines to the Mediterranean.

Syria and Lebanon were finally chosen as the outlets for the pipeline because, as Daniel again revealed, that "would give the United States direct and primary commercial interests in four of the seven Arab states constituting the Arab League and unquestionably exert an influence on Middle Eastern policy."

The amount of money the United States would spend in Syria and Lebanon in building the line, and in operating the outlet (and possibly a refinery) in Lebanon, would be large enough to shape national policy in both countries. It is a bitter pill for France to swallow, but perhaps even more bitter for the British: the latter rushed into the two countries immediately after the war, utilizing the earlier French promise of independence, in an effort to swing this former French sphere into her own camp. Now she is booted out in favor of the United States, for Lebanon will "get enough American dollars in the next four or five years to enable her to declare her financial independence from France." But not from the United States—in the next five years or the foreseeable future.

Daniel adds the routine formula: "and to bulwark the country against Communism," though the native Communist parties are not especially strong and there is no evidence of Soviet influence there at all. But the "anti-Communist" screen inherited from Hitler has a function to perform. It must cover the still more extensive claims to influence and power that the United States is now asserting on the basis of its dominance over the entire oil basin from southern Iran to Syria and from Saudi Arabia to Lebanon. As a minor consequence of "the growth of the American stake in Saudi Arabia and the sheikdoms of Bahrein, Kuweit and Qatar, American influence has increased in Iran," in the form of a financial mission and control of the Iranian gendarmerie, as

Raymond Daniell writes, though he neglects to mention a deal for an American military mission there.

The anti-Communist, anti-Soviet screen has a great deal more than Iran to cover, however. From our dominance of the whole oil area arises a claim to "an essential American interest" in Eastern Europe. And thus we arrive at the Truman Doctrine, the Marshall Plan, the division of the world into two hostile blocs. And no matter how much we scream at Russia, this is of our own doing.

By what logic do we come to claim the right of intervention in Eastern Europe after putting the Near East under our power? By imperialist logic. In his break with the Administration over foreign policy, Henry Wallace, then a member of the Cabinet, said: "We have no more business in the political affairs of Eastern Europe than Russia has in the political affairs of Latin America, Western Europe and the United States." An Administration-inspired *Times* editorial retorted that this "disagreed with Mr. Byrnes' policy of attempting to assert an essential American interest in the political affairs of Eastern Europe."

"Interest?" What "interest?" Cyrus Sulzberger, spokesman for the *Times*-owning Sulzbergers and the business groups they represent, answers the question. "The United States is becoming increasingly aware of its own Mediterranean interests, for Saudi Arabia contains the strategic oil reserve of this country, and Iran, Turkey and Greece virtually comprise a geographical piecrust guarding the anomalous Middle East that contains it." So runs the twisted candor of imperialism: having claimed as "ours" the oil of distant regions and hence the regions themselves, we now assert a "defensive" interest in every country between the oil region and the Soviet Union! Then we set up a deafening clamor about "Soviet expansion" and move into Greece, Turkey and any other country that is not strong enough to kick us out.

"We," of course, do none of this. It is done by "our" oil

barons, our Big Navy imperialists (Admiral Leahy), "our" imperialist "statesmen" like John Foster Dulles, who is simultaneously the legal representative of the biggest private international business and financial interests including German-American combinations. The weak politicians who carry out the policies of the imperialists or who let them be carried out, contract an enormous responsibility before history. But neither can you and I wipe our hands of the matter. In our time, every citizen bears some part of the blame for crimes that he permits to be committed in his name. It is our duty to intervene. The first step is to know the truth and shout it from the housetops.

And the truth — the most important truth of our place and time — is that the United States is expanding at a rate and to an extent never before witnessed by history. While we cry "Stop Thief," at the Soviet Union, we are ourselves engaged in extending what is already the broadest area of military-strategic domination ever controlled by one nation.

CHAPTER 14

CHART OF AMERICAN EMPIRE

How big is the American sphere of influence today? How many square miles and how many millions of people are there in the areas over which the United States today asserts a claim to military-strategic domination? It is time to attempt an answer to this question.

It is no valid objection that American holdings cannot be measured with real precision. Even the difficulty of finding a common denominator for the diverse forms of penetration and influence practised by "advanced" capitalist countries in undeveloped regions, is not an absolute bar to measurement. An approximation of the realities can be achieved.

Such an approximation of the realities of American expansion as might be summed up in a chart or graph, would have at least one firm virtue: it would reduce to ridicule the propaganda myth of a "contracting" sphere of American influence. As for its lack of exactness, a graph or chart is a kind of definition and no worse than any other definition. Definitions are harmful when taken for descriptions of the whole rich, complicated and variegated truth of life itself; they are helpful and useful when employed for limited and clearly defined purposes.

With these reservations, it is proper to begin here a tabulation of American holdings abroad for the purpose of summing up the thesis of this book, namely, that American expansion today unsettles the world. The assertion of military power characterizes American policy today and it is therefore logical to use military-strategic domination as the deciding factor. Of course, potential resistance in many regions may easily prove greater than the strength the

United States can throw into such regions, and no doubt American domination will prove an illusion there at the first test. But that is beside the point here. It is the *assertion* of American supremacy everywhere that prevents a realistic peace settlement.

A tabulation of square miles of land and water, and of millions of people, in areas now under American military-strategic domination, does not represent American expansion in World War II alone. To measure recent expansion, we must deduct the veiled and open possessions of the United States as of 1939.

As early as 1902, a truly classic work (John Atkinson Hobson's, *Imperialism: a Study*) listed the United States among the thirteen imperialist countries. These great powers were conservatively shown to hold one hundred and thirty-six colonies with an area seven times that of the United States and a subject population of more than five hundred millions. The American share was listed as but six colonies, approximately 170,000 square miles in area and with some ten million inhabitants.

In the interest of strict accuracy, it should be observed that the figures represent a somewhat larger American holding, at that period, than would appear at first glance. At any rate, the colonial population is relatively large in proportion to the population of the United States, for the latter was but 77,000,000 at the time.

By 1926, it was conceded that United States formal possessions did not fully define the American Empire. The latter included certain veiled possessions. Professor Parker Thomas Moon of Columbia University made a new tabulation for his *Imperialism and World Politics,* a conservative and apologetic work compared to Hobson's study, but providing more information on American holdings. The American Empire as shown by Moon in 1926, is substantially the American Empire as it stood in 1939. I have reduced his figures to round numbers.

CHART OF AMERICAN EMPIRE BEFORE WORLD WAR II

	Area	Population
OUTLYING TERRITORIES		
Alaska	590,000 sq. miles	60,000
Hawaii	6,500	300,000
DEPENDENCIES		
Philippine Islands	115,000	11,000,000
Puerto Rico	3,500	1,350,000
Virgin Islands	130	26,000
Samoa	60	8,000
Guam	210	13,000
Wake and Midway Islands	30	—
LEASED TERRITORY		
Panama Canal Zone		
Guantanamo (in Cuba)		
Fonseca Bay (Nicaragua)		
Corn Islands (off Nicaragua)	530	27,000
NOMINALLY INDEPENDENT DEPENDENCIES		
Cuba	45,000	3,400,000
Haiti	11,000	2,000,000
Dominican Republic	20,000	900,000
Panama	35,000	450,000
Nicaragua	50,000	650,000
Liberia	35,000	1,500,000
	911,960	21,684,000

In round numbers, the pre-war American Empire, aside from the United States itself, contained 900,000 square miles and twenty-two million inhabitants, compared to the 170,000 square miles and ten million inhabitants shown by Hobson at the turn of the century. As already indicated, far more extensive territories had been earmarked for eventual American control. Neither Hobson nor Moon, moreover, list as empire-territory such countries as China, which were admittedly far from true independence. Where two or more powers contested supremacy, the victim state might theoretically preserve a measure of political independence by playing one rival against the other. In practice, however, the rivals appeared able to maintain a joint dominance and exploitation of major backward countries even while disputing among themselves the division of the spoils. In 1902 or in 1926, therefore, inclusion or exclusion of China from such a list might equally be justified. In 1946, the world is one, and there is no escape for its Chinas.

The world is one to a degree that has completely altered the basis of independence for small nations and large weak ones. Above all, the globe is strategically one, and it is toward this concept that the United States appears to direct its expansion. In the path of the drive, such countries as China have lost the power to zigzag and profit from the differences of rival imperialists. There is no longer a major Anglo-American contest in China; the whole land, but not China's great dependencies — Manchuria and Mongolia — is in the American sphere of interest, influence and power.*

The reasoning that perhaps led Hobson to exclude China from his 1902 chart of empire, no longer holds. But it may be transferred to parts of Europe today where, despite many new American interests, American supremacy may hardly be claimed. American positions that add up to a challenge of British supremacy, therefore, have been indicated but they have not been included in the tabulation of areas and populations under American domination. Inclusion of almost the entire Western Hemisphere and Pacific Ocean areas, in the American sphere, follows the evidence adduced in the early chapters.

---

* *Note to third edition:* Earlier editions warned that the Chinese must be expected to challenge this American claim, and it now appears that the coming year will take much of China proper out of the American sphere.

AMERICAN STRATEGIC EMPIRE AFTER WORLD WAR II

(All figures have been rounded to the nearest five thousand.)

1. WESTERN HEMISPHERE — Sphere of Special Influence and area of absolute strategic domination.

	Area	Population
NORTH AMERICA		
Alaska (possession)	585,000	75,000
Canada	3,700,000	11,500,000
Newfoundland	45,000	315,000
Labrador	110,000	5,000
MIDDLE AMERICA		
Mexico	765,000	20,625,000
Panama	35,000	635,000
Canal Zone (possession)	x	50,000
Costa Rica	25,000	705,000
Salvador	15,000	1,895,000
British Honduras	10,000	65,000
Honduras	45,000	1,105,000
Nicaragua	60,000	1,015,000
Guatemala	45,000	3,450,000
Cuba	45,000	4,780,000
Haiti	10,000	3,000,000
Dominican Republic	20,000	1,825,000
Puerto Rico (possession)	5,000	1,870,000
Virgin Islands (possession)	x	25,000
British West Indies, (Bahamas, Barbados, Jamaica, Leewards, Windwards, Caymans, Trinidad, Tobago)	15,000	2,450,000

SOUTH AMERICA

Colombia	45,000	9,525,000
Venezuela	350,000	3,840,000
British Guiana	90,000	365,000
Dutch Guiana	55,000	180,000
French Guiana	35,000	30,000
Brazil	3,275,000	44,460,000
Uruguay	70,000	2,185,000
Paraguay	175,000	1,040,000
Bolivia	540,000	3,535,000
Peru	530,000	7,025,000
Ecuador	275,000	3,085,000
Chile	295,000	5,235,000
Argentina (excluded)	x	x
Hemisphere Totals	11,070,000	134,995,000

---

2. ATLANTIC THEATER — water area, 26,495,000 square miles in U. S. sphere.

	Area	Population
Greenland	735,000	20,000
Iceland	40,000	125,000
Azores	x	230,000
Ascension	x	x
Bermudas	x	30,000
Liberia	45,000	1,500,000
Atlantic Totals	820,000	1,905,000

(The area of the Atlantic is over 40,000,000 square miles. I have taken the Air Force figure of 26,495,000 for the area covered by our airbase chain as the measure of our water-surface control. This sins on the conservative side.)

3. PACIFIC THEATER — 70,000,000 square miles water area, wholly in U. S. sphere.

	Area	Population
Aleutians (possession)	5,000	x
Hawaii (possession)	5,000	465,000
Philippines	115,000	16,350,000
American Samoas	x	15,000
Wake, Midway, Kure, Howland, Jarvis, Baker, Guam, etc., prewar island possessions, negligible pop., area	x	x
Ryukyu Archipelago, 55 islands	x	575,000
Bonins, 27 islands, Volcanos, including Iwo Jima, three islands	x	5,000
British mandates under U. S. domination	25,000	460,000
New Zealand mandates as above	x	65,000
Australian mandates, principally U. S. base at Manus, New Guinea; Papua	185,000	1,005,000
Japanese Mandates: Marshalls, Marianas or Ladrones, Carolines, Palaus	x	85,000
French Oceania: New Caledonia; Society Islands (Tahiti, etc.) ..	10,000	95,000
Pacific Totals	345,000	19,120,000

4. ASIA

	Area	Population
Japan, direct rule	150,000	72,875,000
China (excluding Manchuria), military, economic, political tutelage and direct strategic domination	2,280,000	422,710,000
Formosa, apparently permanent strategic control	15,000	5,210,000
Korea, half Korean area and population to U. S. sphere ..	45,000	11,000,000
Asia Totals	2,490,000	511,795,000

TOTALS

	Area		
	Water	Land	Population
Western Hemisphere		11,070,000	134,995,000
Atlantic	26,495,000	820,000	1,905,000
Pacific	70,000,000	345,000	19,120,000
Asia		2,490,000	511,795,000
Total Empire	96,495,000	14,725,000	667,815,000
Pre-War Empire		—900,000	—22,000,000
Total Expansion	96,495,000	13,825,000	645,815,000

Thus in the course of World War II, the United States acquired or consolidated de facto dominion over 96,495,000 square miles of ocean and put in claims to domination and control of 13,825,000 square miles of land with 645,815,000 inhabitants. The bulk of this population is not merely dwelling in territory strategically dominated by the United States but is largely included in the military projects of American strategic planners. These figures represent expansion alone. Adding pre-war possessions and early veiled empire, the strategic dominion of the United States as indicated by its military or other de facto controls, extends to 14,725,000 square miles outside our own borders and embraces a population of 667,815,000 "subjects."

Square miles and population figures can give only a formal and limited view of the truly involved relationships in the world power arena. But it is also true that the preceding tabulation has been very cautious, perhaps overly cautious. No statistical accounting has been attempted of American influence aggressively asserted in such decisive strategic areas as Europe, North Africa, the Mediterranean, Central Africa, the Near East, South Asia. The many American positions in those areas — Greece, for instance, now so clearly in the American sphere — have been omitted from the tabulation of land, sea and population control held by the United States as a result of World War II and just as much under digestion as the positions in the chart.

There are areas in which the American advantage is not so patently decisive and yet is great enough to convince realists of American pre-dominance. When eight United States warships were visiting Portugal to back up a demand for American privileges in the Azores, Turner Catledge interviewed dictator Salazar for the *Times*. Unmindful of the care with which the "moral" view of foreign policy is fostered in America, Dr. Salazar blurted out "that Portugal definitely is in the United States sphere of influence" as a result of recent American expansion. He ought to know.

At the opposite end of the Euro-Asiatic landmass — and the opposite political pole from the clerical-Fascist "New State" ruled by Salazar — the American journalist Anna Louise Strong interviewed Mao Tze Tung, Chinese Communist leader, in the Red China capital of Yenan. With matches, cigarettes, teacups and little white winecups, Mao "drew" a map on a small table. Then he described the "map" in these terms:

"In the Pacific, America now controls more than all the former British sphere of influence. . . . She controls China, Japan, half Korea and the South Pacific. She controls also the Near East and Western Europe and Canada and most of South America. . . . America, not Russia, takes Britain's bases, markets, influence-spheres. . . . All these air bases and naval bases that America sets up all over the world . . . are on other people's territory, in Iceland, in Arabia, in China, in other places that do not entirely want them."

Halfway between Lisbon and Yenan lies Ankara whence, in a dispatch July 4, 1948, *Times* correspondent C. L. Sulzberger reported an American military mission under General Horace McBride spending the $100,000,000 Truman Doctrine grant to train and equip the Turkish armed forces and to build strategic roads (to the Soviet border).

"Members of the United States Army group are permitted to travel all over the country and are told whatever they wish to know by the Turkish General Staff . . . General McBride's mission is working together with a British training mission that has been in Turkey considerably longer. . . . However, *there is no doubt that the United States has the paramount position.*"

Thus the reality beyond the chart is this: the United States seeks literally global strategic hegemony. Whether you and I like it or not, we are engaged in boundless expansion. The counter-pressure of other powers and the resistance of the peoples manipulated and injured by our domination, will eventually either set limits to our outward thrust or cause our empire to burst at the seams. But in the meantime, it is a fact that the United States has not, of its own volition, set any bounds whatsoever to its aspiration for power. Nor is either of the two major political parties demanding such limitation.

Who remembers the Democratic national platform in the great campaign of 1900? It said:

"We assert that no nation can long endure half republic and half empire, and we warn the American people that imperialism abroad will lead quickly and inevitably to despotism at home."

PART III: TAKE YOUR CHOICE

CHAPTER 15

THE PRICE OF REACTION

The warning of the 1900 Democratic platform is even more timely today that it was in that first wave of American imperialist expansion half a century ago. Our fate at home turns on our role in the world. If we do not force the imperialists to reverse the program we have permitted them to adopt in our name, we will pay as dearly as any other people — or more so — for the greedy gains that reach only a few private interests. We cannot defend or tolerate imperialist expansion, whether under the name of "moral responsibility" or of "world leadership," without bringing down upon our heads war, the militarization and regimentation of the nation, the decay of democracy at home. A ruthless program of world conquest — no matter how prettily described — must have drastic domestic consequences. The first victim of an American drive for empire is the American people.

The peacetime draft, abandoning a 150-year boast of freedom from the burdens of militarism, is one of the costs of empire. The anti-Communist hysteria and the spy hunts, inflation, violence against followers of Henry Wallace as well as against labor, all belong in the same picture. It was no accident that the draft was rushed through in an election year; the demands of empire overbore the protests of the politicians. And by signing the bill at once, whereas he might have waited ten days, President Truman caught up in the draft thousands of young men who would otherwise have been able to enter college for the 1948 Fall session. By his hasty gesture, the President was no doubt clearing up an important point: guns, having already replaced butter, must now replace books!

It is the loss of butter rather than of books, however

that is felt immediately by most people. The workingman just can't make ends meet. And watching the fantastic arms appropriations, he doesn't have to be a master of theory to find a connection between runaway prices and a program of world conquest. A glance at the 1948-1949 budget indicates the relative concern of the bi-partisans with standards of armaments and standards of living. In a forty billion dollar budget that allots eleven billions to "national defense" and seven more to the conduct of our foreign policy (forty-six per cent of the budget) only thirty-seven *millions* were made available for housing. President Truman made a brave show of concern for social welfare in the budget (1948 being an election year) but the *Times,* defending the President from "anti-New Deal" criticism, gave the game away. "The sum total of the cost of the new welfare programs" proposed by the President, said the *Times,* is only $452,000,000; "that is a little more than one per cent of the budget."

Yes, one per cent for social welfare, forty-six per cent for imperialist expansion via militarization. But that's by no means the whole story. The costs of our present course, now estimated in tens of billions of dollars a year, soar beyond control in the face of mounting resistance and mounting inflation. Millions of working people are forced by their daily needs to fight, usually through trade unions, for a little more butter or at least bread. More bread, however, means fewer guns, so the bipartisan expansionists must, by the very nature of their program, take measures to defeat the workingman's demand for higher wages.

The Wall Street clique in command of our nation employs a double offensive to balk working-class resistance to its plans. On the one hand, through such measures as the Taft-Hartley Act, it seeks to destroy or undermine the labor unions. On the other hand, within the unions, under the slogan of anti-Communism, it incites civil war.

The entire domestic program of the Wall Street clique and its bipartisan political front, rests on the anti-Communist hysteria first tested by the Nazis. Many States already have laws designed to outlaw "Communism," and the spy frenzy of the 1948 election campaign indicates that Federal laws of the kind are on their way. Such laws, by denying the right to *advocate* Socialism, obviously abandon the very pretense of democracy. But that is the least of the damage they do. "Anti-Communist" laws are in language so broad that every Wallaceite, every critic of profiteering and warmongering, becomes a "Communist" subject to expulsion from any public or trade union office, and, indeed, to criminal prosecution.

Nor would it make a great difference if the language of the laws were improved. The climate of hysteria and the purpose of the laws coincide with the broad language; they lead to trial by headline and to political ostracism of all who oppose the Wall Street clique. A perfect example of the technique was the indictment of the national leaders of the Communist Party on the eve of the national convention of the new Progressive Party. The charge was that they "conspired" to found a Communist Party! But headlines and the Congressional spy inquiries combined to make it appear that they had been charged with espionage.

The breadth of the language and the depth of the hysteria are alike necessary to the real aims of the Wall Street clique. Under the pretext of "exposing" Communism, they are deliberately attacking fundamental constitutional and human rights in an effort to squelch all opposition. It must be acknowledged that millions of Americans who don't want an empire — especially at the price of inflation now and war and Fascism later — are terrorized into silence at a time when their protests might still halt the stampede. "Terrorized" is not too strong a word. True, we have no formal concentration camps as yet. But active opponents of imperialism are jailed or threatened with jail on "criminal" charges of patent political complexion. The newest trick is to send such men to prison for contempt of the Thomas-Rankin House Committee on un-American Activities. The economic blacklist is an even more potent terror weapon. A reporter, a teacher, a worker, is fired simply because he is a Communist. But it is not Communists alone whose heads fall under this primitive economic guillotine. More than one college teacher lost his job during the 1948 campaign after he publicly announced his support of Henry Wallace. Once you reach the point where the name "Communist" is a justification for any outrage, it is easy to eliminate political opponents by branding them Communist, or to prevent opposition by threatening to call it Communist.

That is the score today. The United States Attorney General decrees that a long list of organizations is subversive and every member of, or contributor to, any of the listed organizations may be considered subversive "by association." We are frequently reminded that the un-American Committee alone has more than a million names in its files. The intended moral is clear: if you don't want to starve or go to jail, don't take the Bill of Rights seriously. Keep your mouth shut, work harder, eat less, scream hurrah every time another billion dollars is thrown to the Army, Navy or Air Force; and, finally, give thanks for Free Enterprise when those very billions turn up on the financial page in the form of record-breaking profits for Big Business.

No, we don't have concentration camps as yet. Nothing so open as that. Instead we have a carefully-nursed hysteria calculated to get the majority of Americans to surrender their civil liberties as a patriotic duty. At the height of the hysteria, it is hoped, they will even join in doing violence to the "extremists" who defend their civil liberties and persist in opposing the drive to war and despotism. And thus, in the name of patriotism, we are promised Storm Troopers, and in the name of "defense of Democracy," we are on our way to — Fascism!

WHO STARTED THE "COLD" WAR?

It is becoming very difficult to conceal this dark prospect. So the men who make our policy have more or less quit trying to conceal it. Their newer tactic is to admit that we have undertaken a costly program that will impose very heavy and unrewarded sacrifices upon the American people. But we did not do this willingly, runs the argument. It was forced upon us. Soviet "faithlessness" to pacts, and Russia's incomprehensible "provocation" of loyal, kindly America, forced the United States—reluctantly and with no selfish objective—to our present "defensive" militarization of the nation. Russia is alone to blame for our hostile attitude toward her. General Marshall, in a speech on November 19, 1947, put it this way:

"There may have been some genuine feeling [by Soviet representatives in the UN General Assembly] that the purposes of this government and the attitude of most of the American press were definitely hostile to the Soviet Union . . . The truth as I see it is that from the termination of hostilities down to the present time the Soviet Government has consistently followed a course which was bound to arouse the resentment of our people . . . So many of the actions of that Government were provocative without any other evident purpose — I have been at a loss to determine why a government should . . . deliberately provoke such animosities as are evident at this time."

The pretense that our present policies have their origin in postwar developments, the assertion that they are a defensive reaction to Russian provocation, won't stand up against the facts. It is flatly against the record. And not the record of the past two years alone, but of the past thirty. The "cold" war didn't start on V-E Day or V-J Day. It started in 1917 when fourteen powers, under the leadership of Winston Churchill, organized an armed intervention designed to overthrow the newly established Soviet regime. The Russians remember that. They also remember that only their publication of secret Anglo-French agreements prevented the multi-power coalition from partitioning Russia. The Ukraine was to be assigned to the French sphere of influence; the areas around the Caspian Sea, including the oil of the Caucausus, was to fall under British domination.

The joint intervention failed in its armed phase but was continued in the political-diplomatic form of the *cordon sanitaire.* In the 1930s it took the form of "appeasement," meaning the appeasing (or, more accurately, the deliberate arming) of a Nazified Germany, with the aim of inducing a mutually destructive German-Russian war. Appeasement went wrong—the Nazis first waged war on the West. Nevertheless, the Western Powers did not cease working to weaken, undermine, and overthrow the Soviet Union. The old game of intervention continued throughout World War II despite the apparent truce marked by the wartime meetings of President Roosevelt, Prime Minister Churchill and Premier Stalin.

Was this simply European politics, or was it universal *capitalist* politics? The role of America shows that it was the latter. We participated in the anti-Soviet game at every stage. Our contribution to the original intervention was typical: we sent food and Herbert Hoover. In Hoover's hands, the food was a more powerful weapon of counterrevolution than the American expeditionary forces which were sent to Murmansk and Siberia. Later, we trailed along on the policy of appeasement, as witness the "Neutrality Law" by which we helped strangle the Spanish Republic. And despite differences between Britain and America, we joined in a common strategy during the early war years (notably the delay of a Western Front in favor of the North African and Italian adventures) that had the effect of letting Russia bleed, as appeasement had intended.

Later in the war, there were still sharper Anglo-American differences, but upon examination they reveal no contradiction of the basic capitalist solidarity against the Soviet Union. Many books and documents published since the war indicate that events convinced President Roosevelt the Socialist State was here to stay; indeed, Stalingrad demonstrated that it was the second-ranking power in today's world. Roosevelt therefore proposed to modify Allied policy with respect to Russia. The record shows that Churchill, backed by many powerful Americans, opposed even that temporary modification. Former Assistant Secretary of State Adolph A. Berle recently revealed that he left the State Department as a result of a fight within the government in 1944. The issue was that his group was unalterably opposed to any "softening" of our line toward Russia even at that peak of wartime collaboration. The British and American anti-Russian bitter-enders opposed the Second Front strategy and the Teheran-Yalta postwar settlements. They held out for a military-political strategy whose principal aim was to continue the secret drive against Russia, during and after the war. As a result they were in no hurry to defeat Germany and Japan, and at all times contemplated their future use in an anti-Soviet front.

Roosevelt, aided by the fact that many expansionist interests felt the United States must participate in the decisive European actions in order to gain a decisive postwar voice, had his way while he lived. The result was one that left a mark on history: a decisive coalition military strategy was followed, and Germany and Japan were crushingly defeated. But the subsequent fate of Mr. Roosevelt's postwar settlements demonstrates how reluctantly the Big Business rulers of our country had participated in the brief honeymoon with Russia. The President's death and the end of the wartime pressure shortly after that unhappy event quickly restored to power the men who had opposed Mr. Roosevelt's wartime strategy and postwar settlements. The truce was over.

It was not immediately possible for Harry Truman, who

succeeded to the presidency, to announce that he was discarding the Roosevelt policies. Indeed Mr. Truman, soon after he took office, confirmed the Yalta-Teheran agreements in a Big Three meeting at Berlin. But Truman was putty in the hands of the imperialists and willing enough, in any event, to carry out their wishes. Nothing more clearly evidenced this willingness than his invitation to Winston Churchill to make the latter's famous speech at Fulton, Missouri, in May 1946. There, in addition to launching the "iron curtain," "police state" and "slave labor" catch-phrases of contemporary anti-Soviet propaganda, Churchill outlined the new anti-Communist "crusade" which was taken over bodily, in March 1947, and "Americanized" under the name of the "Truman Doctrine." The Truman Doctrine, however, is nothing but the old Churchill Doctrine, not just of May 1946 but of November 1917 and all the years between. The Churchill-Truman Doctrine was, in effect, a public promise to break our wartime agreements.

The plan to scrap Potsdam and its Teheran-Yalta predecessors, signified an increasingly open return to the destroy-socialism and overthrow-the-Soviet Union principle of capitalist-socialist relations. To cover up a series of progressively bolder steps in this direction, the new policy-makers (just as the old enemies of President Roosevelt) launched a great blame-it-on-Russia propaganda campaign. More and more clearly, the drive to scrap the wartime settlement with Russia was coupled with a scheme to rebuild Germany and Japan, drive the Soviet Union out of the United Nations and organize the latter against Russia. More and more the hate-Russia campaign was accompanied by an insistence on our right to intervene anywhere in the world, by force of arms, where socialism appeared likely to gain favor. Indeed, that is the substance of the Truman Doctrine and of its offspring, the Marshall Plan.

The men who argue that we became anti-Soviet only because the Russians broke the agreements, say that with tongue in cheek. Senator Arthur Vandenberg, initiator of the "get tough with Russia" line, was once asked "if our new bipartisan American foreign policy no longer follows the Franklin D. Roosevelt pattern." He replied:

"Well, that depends what you mean by the 'Roosevelt pattern.' If you mean the 'Roosevelt pattern' as originally laid down in the Atlantic Charter, I should say that we are earnestly seeking to return to it after it was partially scrapped by the late President himself at Yalta."

John Foster Dulles, Republican foreign policy expert and widely regarded as the real Secretary of State behind General Marshall dotted the i's on Vandenberg's remarks. Said Dulles, "We are never going back to Teheran or Yalta."

Some of the Roosevelt-haters won't bother to pretend that Russia violated the wartime settlements. On the contrary, they boast of American repudiation. *Barron's Magazine,* bible of Wall Street, writes: "We might claim that in throwing overboard Yalta and Teheran, and boldly rewriting Potsdam, we are bypassing the errors of fifteen years," (*i.e.,* the "error" of recognizing Russia in the first place).

THE MARSHALL PLAN

So much for the spurious Russia-broke-faith theme. A companion piece is the propagandistic use of the Marshall Plan to justify our aggressive policies and our world expansion. The Marshall Plan argument runs like this:

"We tried to pacify the world and restore the basis of well-being by putting the world back on its feet. We sought nothing for ourselves, it was the greatest piece of altruism the world has ever seen, the very opposite of imperialism. And despite Russian and Communist attempts to sabotage this plan, we are still trying and intend to carry it out. We are only showing strength so that the plan will get a chance to put 'like-minded' countries on their feet where they can defend themselves. Then everything will calm down, Russia won't be tempted by other people's weakness to engage in new adventures, and democracy (or at least capitalism) will be saved."

The main trouble with this argument is that it depends upon an utterly false characterization of the Marshall Plan. Neither in origin, concépt nor operation is the Marshall Plan disinterested; it does not and cannot put the European participating states "on their feet." On the contrary, it was designed to further the present United States policy of expansion at the expense of the independence of European and other states.

Such charges are anticipated and dismissed by the familiar device of calling them "Communist." When I briefly characterized the plan, in the first edition of this book, as a scheme to "colonize" Europe, reviewer Hans Kohn, in the *Times* book section, wearily waved that away as the "party line."* But come now, Professor Kohn, is it really just Moscow and the Communists who see in the Marshall Plan a selfish scheme for the benefit of American Big Business? Are there no other parties that "profess" to see infiltration, penetration, domination and exploitation by American private interests and by the United States under cover of the plan? I believe I can find evidence that the whole non-Communist world sees it that way, and I will look no farther than the pages of the *Times* itself, my dear professor.

Item. A dispatch from Geneva by Michael L. Hoffman, dated July 30. Said Hoffman: "**The fact is that many of the** things the Russians said about the European Recovery Program are being said very loudly at present by respectable non-Communist opinion in almost every Western European country.

"This is the case with charges of United States interference in domestic affairs through the control of the use of local currency proceeds of Marshall Plan imports, of United

---

* See page 38.

States business penetration under the cloak of that plan, of United States determination to bind Europe to the continued importation of certain commodities of which the United States has threatening surpluses."

Item. Another dispatch from Geneva by Hoffman, July 3, 1948, headed: "ECA NATIONS FEAR U.S. INTERFERENCE."

"No amount of argument can convince the general run of Europeans that, while ERP is broadly what it purports to be—an expression of enlightened American self-interest in stabilizing Europe—there won't be a goodly number of plums pulled out of the pie by big American companies in the form of property, markets and commitments of European governments to keep hands off their operations."

As more than a fifth of the whole Marshall Plan "aid" to Europe is oil, that's one plum of watermelon size. Some half-dozen American oil giants share it.

Gather and collate news items for a few days and you will see that they document this definition. Some of these dispatches relate how a committee of American Big Businessmen demands an end to British subsidies that "keep the working class cost of living down," because "when the worker doesn't have to pay much for food he isn't as interested as he should be in working harder to get more pay." Others relate how the unpatriotic and feeble ruling classes of Europe are eager to increase American control of their domestic affairs: they want the United States to police their countries and maintain their power. And running through all the dispatches is the evidence that the whole world thinks —and says—of the Marshall Plan what only the Communists are supposed to say: that it operates to subjugate, Europe and European dependencies, to the will of a small number of powerful Americans.

Item. Harold Callender, reporting from Paris July 31, 1948, makes this bland admission:

"While European Foreign Ministers and others speak publicly of the United States' generosity in aiding Europe they are more likely to speak privately of the politically embarrassing control that United States officials feel obliged to impose upon every major European measure taken to carry out the Marshall Plan.

"This claim to the right to control and check is seized upon to support Moscow's argument that the Marshall Plan is designed to destroy the independence of European states and it disturbs even Winston Churchill. . . ."

It had to be that way. The Marshall Plan in practice cannot be better than the Marshall Plan in principle. In the chronological and historical record the plan is revealed as an integral part of contemporary American foreign policy. And what kind of loan policy could serve a basic policy of boundless economic expansion by American private interests? What kind of loan policy could be consistent with boundless political-strategic expansion by the United States? The answer is the Marshall Plan—an expansionist policy with military trimmings.

The Marshall Plan became, under the fancy title of European Recovery Program, a special effort to conquer positions in Europe in the context of our world expansion. In its working out, the plan passed from a system of loans with political strings, to direct day-to-day supervision of European internal affairs by Americans. While making more or less progress toward creating a war alliance of the Marshall Plan states, it seeks to reduce Europe to uniform financial dependence upon the United States, helpless economic subordination to Wall Street, shameful political subservience to Washington.

"BLUNDERING" TO WAR

This then, is the monstrosity called the Marshall Plan. It turns out to be nothing more than false whiskers failing to conceal the familiar features of the Churchill-Truman

Doctrine. Insofar as this doctrine rests chiefly on hatred of the Soviet Union, today's imperialists might well heed the warning dropped in 1915 by Henry Cabot Lodge, chairman of the Senate Foreign Relations Committee. "Animosity is no policy," said Lodge. American policy is more, however, than anti-Sovietism. Recognized everywhere as a program of world expansion, it meets with worldwide resistance. More and more, it depends for its enforcement upon use of force and constant show of force, which in turn bring new resistance. Thus a situation is created in which there is an hourly invitation to war but instead of altering that artificial situation, our policy-makers treat it as natural and ask us to bear all the burdens of unlimited armaments that it imposes. The report of the President's Air Policy Commission in January 1948, puts it this way:

"On first impression it might seem that a major war during Phase I [before 1952 when other powers are considered first likely to have developed the atom bomb] is unlikely, and this opinion has been expressed to the commission by high military authorities. There is, however, such a thing as blundering into a war . . ."

There is no better way to blunder into a war than to adopt a policy that makes you dependent upon generals and admirals. And that is what we have done. We first claim just about the whole globe as a "vital national interest" of the United States, then declare our intention, as in the same report, "of arming the United States so strongly that other nations will hesitate to attack us or our vital national interests." Non-conformity with American views on Greece, Iran, China, the Arctic or the Antarctic becomes an "attack on our vital national interests."

Protection of such wide-ranging "interests" under a formula that broad, dictates our further behavior. In public documents and actions, we announce that we won't consider the United States adequately armed until we have taken up positions all over the globe and organized all the rest of the world against the Soviet Union. Committed to such a policy, the civilian elements in the government must lean heavily on the military men, giving the latter free rein. Thereupon the generals and admirals begin to bluster and threaten, employing the sabre-rattling "diplomacy" so natural to the militarist.

Almost daily, we see exhibitions of that kind, performances that cannot be described in milder terms than those I have used. An example is the final report of Admiral Nimitz, retiring as chief of naval operations. After declaring that the United States has "absolute" command of the seas, Nimitz said:

"The net result is that [our] naval forces are able, without resorting to diplomatic channels, to establish offshore anywhere in the world, air fields . . . virtually as complete as any air base ever established."

The report fully conformed to the war-inviting official theory of American security according to which we can be safe only if we are prepared, at a moment's notice and from the very borders of Russia, to launch utterly destructive attacks upon every city in the Soviet Union. Nimitz duly described the Navy's strategy of "mobile" air fields as a system of "offensive bases" from which to raid a land easily identified as Russia. And he specifically included atomic bomb attacks from carrier-based planes as part of the program.

Call that preparedness, if you will, but to be logical you must then be prepared to admit that Russian preparedness requires not just special positions in her borderlands, but air bases and naval bases in this hemisphere, in the islands of the Atlantic and Pacific, in the Caribbean Sea, in Canada and Mexico. She cannot be safe until she is prepared, at the first blow from the United States, to raze Detroit and St. Louis as well as New York and San Francisco. To admit the logic of this counter-demand, is to recognize the illogic of an armaments race even in the sacred name of "security."

It is not preparedness, it is browbeating, blustering, provocation. Say, if you will, that such conduct risks "blundering to war," but then you might equally say of a man who carefully soaks the ground around a house with gasoline and throws a lighted match into the yard, that he "risks" setting the house on fire. And everything flows from this. There is no possibility of correctly deciding what must be done today, unless one boldly faces the fact that United States policy, not Soviet policy, lights the flames of war.

Who threatens whom? Though one were to haggle over each day's stories of power-rivalry in Hungary or Korea, one thing about Soviet positions—as compared with American positions — stands out for any schoolboy from any map: the Soviet positions are close to home. They never bring Russian arms substantially nearer to the United States. But American positions are another matter. In China we are on the Soviet border itself, and so we are in Iran and in Turkey (where a loan or gift of submarines is for the announced purpose of operation in the Black Sea.) In Japan, Korea and, for that matter, the Philippines, we are within direct invasion range of Russia. In Saudi Arabia, all through the Mediterranean, northern Canada, and the so-called "Atlantic community," there is no way of interpreting our positions as "defensive." They are not only aggressive, threatening, menacing to the Soviet Union, but our authorities are at great pains to emphasize that intent.

Who threatens whom? No Soviet spokesman has ever been heard calling for preventive war on the United States. But a host of prominent Americans, including high public officials, have openly advocated that we atom-bomb Russia now. As Hanson Baldwin wrote in the *Times* on October 4, 1948:

"Since the war not only the civilian leaders of the military establishment, but uniformed officers themselves have been most vocal about foreign affairs. Their judgments and pronunciamentos have been so frequent and emphatic . . . that sometimes one would suspect that the military, and not the State Department, was making foreign policy. . . .

"General George C. Kenney of the Air Force, General Carl Spaatz, lately Chief of Staff of the Air Force, and a host of other military people have been speaking and writing openly about war with the Soviet Union and about attacking it with atomic bombs. . . . Secretary of the Air Force W. Stuart Symington [has] described the possibilities of the trans-polar bombardment of the Soviet Union.

"Last week [Secretary of the Navy, John L.] Sullivan and [Secretary of the Army, Kenneth C.] Royall in two public speeches made strong attacks on the Soviet Union. Mr. Royall's was the most blatant and aggressive—and the least excusable. . . . He castigated the Soviet Union by calling her leaders 'international shysters.'

"Such language and such an address during a domestic political campaign and at a time of delicate international tension would seem to indicate irresponsibility. It is language that can do no good whatsoever and is certain to do much harm. It is the language of war . . . [That] language has now become such a commonplace it attracts little attention. . . . The United States has reached a psychological frame of mind—dangerous in the extreme—that can, in itself, be a cause for war."

Why does Baldwin think militaristic talk more dangerous than militaristic actions? The recent announcement of a draft military alliance between Canada and the United States, to lead to "a seven-nation unified military and strategic command under an American Commander in Chief," and with an American "right to establish air, land or sea bases in any of the five countries," would seem deadly to peace.

It is not the militarists alone, however, who contribute in one way or another to warmongering. It was the relatively pacific scientist, Professor Harold Urey, who long ago suggested that we "may have" to start an atomic war "with the frank purpose of conquering the world and ruling it as we desire, and preventing any other nation from developing mass weapons of war." And the American delegation to the United Nations, including Mrs. Eleanor Roosevelt, has steadfastly refused to disavow or criticize a warmonger who happens to be an American citizen. Mrs. Roosevelt, in answer to a question I put to her, confirmed that this was the considered policy of the delegation—and presumably of the United States government.

Mrs. Roosevelt is not a warmonger; Dr. Urey is not one of our outstanding Hitler-minded incendiaries. Their positions are shocking precisely because they do not derive from personal inclination; they follow rather the unconscious logic of American policy today: a world drive for power coupled with fierce self-righteousness. If we begin with a presumed monopoly of both morality and the A-bomb, we are almost compelled to force the rest of the world to accept peace on our terms. And if, out of their moral backwardness, some peoples resist this *Pax Americana,* we can redeem them with atom bombs.

Not Professor Urey and Mrs. Roosevelt alone, but most Americans, may find it hard to believe that we are not the purest of disinterested nations. Let us look, however, at just one fact that might make a European, an African, a South American or an Asiatic reluctant to concede our moral perfection. How did we use the first A-bomb? The documents released by President Truman and others show that we made a cold-blooded decision to bomb a "dual target, that is, a military installation or war plant *surrounded by or adjacent to houses* and other buildings most susceptible to damage!" With all our high morality, we deliberately and by careful pre-decision atom-bombed civilians! For their own good, no doubt.

CHAPTER 16

THERE IS A WAY

The kind of mind capable of making the "dual" target decision when the first atomic bomb was dropped, is not capable of making the contrary decision—to abandon atomic diplomacy and let the world quiet down. An unnamed but authoritative American spokesman, commenting on the Moscow negotiations in September 1948, said it was foolish to think the American-Soviet deadlock would be resolved in the foreseeable future. The crisis isn't going to end, he told newsmen. "The American people will just have to get used to it."

Of course, if you're willing to live in a state of perpetual siege, you won't care how long minds like that govern our country. But you probably do care. You are probably far from convinced of the theory, pithily expressed in the headline about Ernest Bevin's speech to the UN General Assembly on September 27, 1948: "Russia To Blame If Atomic War Breaks Out." You would like to do something to keep it from breaking out.

It takes no genius to see that the way to start is to get rid of the men who are now militarizing America, setting up United States bases in all parts of the earth and organizing most of the world into anti-Soviet blocs and *de facto* war alliances. We will have to dislodge the bankers, generals and admirals before we can rid ourselves of their policies.

Agreed. But who will bell the cat? Who will drive the "Wall Street-military team" out of Washington? Or, to put the question more constructively, *how* shall we—you and I, the whole American people—do this job that so obviously needs doing? The relatively recent birth and remarkable growth of the new Progressive Party promises to supply an answer. The peace program of the new party has won a quick following because it goes to the heart of the problem. As expressed in the party platform, adopted July 23-25, 1948, at the founding convention of the new party: "The root cause of this crisis is Big Business control of our economy and government." As spelled out in succeeding paragraphs of that document:

We have built "the world's greatest productive machine," only to see its ownership "concentrated in the hands of a few and its product used for their enrichment." Through possession of this economic power, the owners have established a private political power, "an invisible government which pulls the strings of its puppet Republican and Democratic parties. Two sets of candidates compete for votes under the outworn emblems of the old parties. But both represent a single program—a program of monopoly profits through war preparations, lower living standards, and suppression of dissent."

In willing obedience to "the dictates of monopoly and the military," the two old parties therefore "prepare for war in the name of peace. They refuse to negotiate a settlement with the Soviet Union." They misuse the United Nations and "use the Marshall Plan to rebuild Nazi Germany as a war base and to subjugate the economies of other European countries to American Big Business. They finance and arm corrupt, fascist governments. . . . They encircle the globe with military bases which other peoples cannot but view as threats to their freedom and security. They protect the war-making industrial and financial barons of Nazi Germany and imperial Japan, and restore them to power. They stockpile atomic bombs. . . . They fill policy-making positions with generals and Wall Street bankers."

The Progressive Party proposes, in effect, to expel from Washington the men and parties responsible for this state of affairs. Its program expresses the conviction "that the brotherhood of man can be achieved and the scourge of war ended." It rejects "anti-Soviet hysteria as a mask for monopoly, militarism and reaction," and holds that "a return to the purpose of Franklin Roosevelt to seek areas of international agreement rather than disagreement," is the key "to the organization of world peace. . . . If peace is to be achieved capitalist United States and Communist Russia must establish good relations and work together. . . ."

The letter Henry Wallace wrote to President Truman on July 23, 1946, when Mr. Wallace was still in the Cabinet, remains a valid statement of the way to end the cold war: "We should ascertain from a fresh point of view what Russia believes to be essential to her own security as a prerequisite to the writing of the peace and to cooperation in the construction of a world order. We should be prepared to judge her requirements against the background of what we ourselves and the British have insisted upon as essential to our respective security. We should be prepared, even at the expense of risking epithets of appeasement, to agree to reasonable Russian guarantees of security."

There is nothing in these suggestions that the average American would find unreasonable. But the average American does not make the policies pursued by the United States government. We began our discussion by noting that the Lamonts, du Ponts, Rockefellers and Mellons are the real policy-makers of our country. We also saw, however, that they rule only by default. If the Progressive Party proves a permanent growing movement and its program a guide to continuous battle rather than a mere electoral document, it can become a popular current strong enough to change the course of the American ship of state.

It may be that history will reject that appraisal as over-optimistic. It may be that the present program and composition of the Progressive Party will prove inadequate to today's needs or tomorrow's crises. Big Business employs increasingly brutal methods, rapidly degenerating into organized violence, to prevent any party from bringing the real issues of our time before the American people. It may be that only a movement consciously committed to Socialism and basing itself on the toughness and consistency of the working class, will prove strong enough to cope with the concentrated power ruthlessly exercised by the tremendous monopolies centered in Wall Street.

But these are questions that can wait. We who believe that capitalism itself constantly works to produce monopoly, need not quarrel over questions of theory with the Wallace-ites who want to fight the monopolists while preserving the capitalism that creates and recreates them each day. The vital thing today is that we fight side by side against the recognized enemy—the Big Business despots and their bipartisan warmongers—for a program that gives the great masses of Americans a chance to learn politics by doing. That describes the Progressive Party and its program. Because it holds out the promise of assisting the American people to fight for their civil rights, defend their standards of living and organize for peace and security, the Progressive Party is the most hopeful development in America today.

The real problem is not the possible inadequacy of the Progressive Party; it is the problem of breaking through the domestic iron curtain to rouse millions of Americans to the dangers before us and the source of those dangers. People everywhere else in the world are able to recognize the hand of Wall Street and that protects them from easy acceptance of our "moral" propaganda. But it is much more important—to us, at least—that the majority of the American people fully grasp the situation.

In our time, stubborn persistence in the course the United States is following, can only lead to the decline of the American nation. It may be hard for Americans to accept the historical possibility of the future decay of America, just as it is difficult for most Britons to recognize that the great British Empire has already crumbled away with no great new British Socialist Federation to replace it. Yet if we in America are not to go through a far worse experience we shall have to take America off the path of imperialism. And to start with, we shall have to learn how to recapture control of our foreign policy from the brutal and inept imperialists who have the helm today.

To call them inept is somewhat misleading. True, they make crude tactical blunders in the execution of their policy. But the really glaring "mistakes" they commit are not the result of their own inadequacy but of the general hopelessness of the goal they pursue. Men who undertake to build a world empire in the era of the visible decay of empire, cannot avoid making ridiculous decisions. So our bipartisans, with the best brains of Wall Street guiding them, can do no better, in choosing allies, than the contemptible Greek Royalists, the medieval Chiang Kai Shek, and latterly, it would appear, Frau Ilse Koch who made lampshades from the skins of Nazi victims at Buchenwald.

If hopelessly weak allies are one result of a historically hopeless policy, the backing of successive lost causes is another. American arms are being sent—it is a matter of official admissions and undenied reports—to the imperialist slavemasters in Burma, Malaya, Indonesia, Indo-China, and everywhere else that the tide of liberty has reached the flood of revolt. In the United Nations, too, it is impossible to conceal the American role, for on colonial issues every vote finds the United States with Britain, France, Holland and Belgium against not just the Soviet Union and its allies but a long list of UN states that have known (or still know) the meaning of colonialism.

Surely the bipartisans know they are backing a losing horse? Inevitably the colonial peoples will win. It is clear that they *are* winning, and that together with the millions of people who have turned toward Socialism or have positively rejected capitalism, they are too strong to be put down by any combination imperialism can create. With the hard fact of the existence of the Soviet Union, as a starting point, they too are capable of adding up the forces on both sides. The Soviet Union, the new Socialist-bound countries of Eastern Europe, the tens of millions of people in non-Socialist countries who are actively fighting for Socialism, the scores of millions of colonials and semi-colonials who automatically turn to the Soviet Union for aid in their struggles even when they are under anti-Communist and anti-Soviet influence, all these add up to the decisive force in the world today.

The Wall Street clique and its bipartisan political agents have elected to put down these millions who are on the march. Aside from counting upon its ability to use us in any conflict, the clique seeks allies everywhere—and comes up with those we have described. It is an idiot's dream. The bipartisans can lead us only to war—and defeat in war, at that—to helplessness in the face of the problems presented by modern life, to deep stagnation in the backwash of history. If we follow that path, other lands and peoples will take up the task of world leadership. They will, no doubt, direct international life toward a world society of equal peoples, a society in which man will cease to drift helplessly toward war and crisis but will assert increasing, planned control of his own destiny.

In the end we, or what is left of us, will also benefit from such a development. But why should we first drift through war and crisis, to ruin and decay? Why should we not at once throw the weight of the United States, with its unmatched productive power, into the scales of history on the side of history? Then indeed we would not risk the decline of a great nation but would assume a world leadership that no one anywhere could or would wish to challenge. The Wall Street bipartisans will not and cannot lead us in the direction of our choice. But it is nowhere written by the finger of God on tablets of stone that we must let the imperialists run our country forever.